VERSTEHEN:
Subjective Understanding in the Social Sciences

Edited by

MARCELLO TRUZZI
New College, Sarasota, Florida

ADDISON-WESLEY PUBLISHING COMPANY

Reading, Massachusetts
Menlo Park, California
London • Don Mills, Ontario

This book is in the
Addison-Wesley Series in
Dialogues in the Social Sciences

Consulting Editor
Marcello Truzzi

Contents

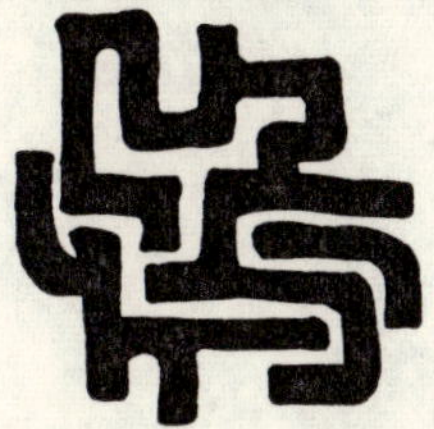

Introduction

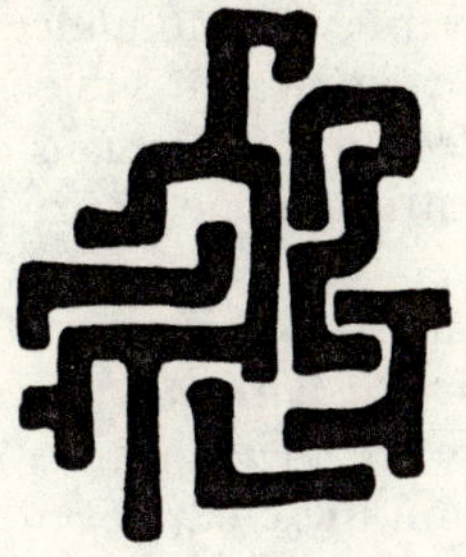

A basic issue throughout the history of the social sciences has been the character and limitations of their explanatory goals. On one side of this issue have been those who followed the positivistic Father of Sociology, Auguste Comte (1798 - 1857), envisaging the social sciences as basically (methodologically) no different from the natural sciences. The same sorts of reasoning, method, and explanatory role were seen to characterize the social and the natural sciences. Social facts, like physical facts, were said to be equally real, equally empirical, and equally measurable, and it was believed that their study would ultimately generate the same kinds of law-like propositions and explanatory coverage believed to be present in the natural sciences.

On the other side of the issue, which originated largely from the writings of the philosopher-historian Wilhelm Dilthey, were those who argued that a basic distinction exists between physical events (such as those investigated in the natural sciences) and man's social actions, which are the focus of attention in the social sciences. The latter were seen as meaningful forms of activity not only to the scientist-observer but to the subjects-actors themselves; and these meaningful elements in action, they argued, account greatly for the variations one observes in man's behavior. For these "humanistic" antipositivistic thinkers, the social or cultural sciences are of a character basically and radically different from that of the natural sciences. This difference necessitates a concern for the subjective states of men, a concern with interpreting and understanding men's motives and cognitions. This process of subjective interpretation (*verstehen*, as it was called by the Germans who initiated this debate) was seen as an essential and necessary part of the development of a social science.

Within these two rather polarized positions, which we are loosely calling the *positivistic-naturalistic* versus the *humanistic-culturalistic* camps, there are a wide variety of subpositions. Within the naturalistic tradition there have been two prominent perspectives toward the role of subjective understanding. At one extreme we have the hard-line positivists who deny the importance of such subjective data as explanatory constructs or who flatly consider such a concern to be antiscientific because, they argue, such claims in the past have never been capable of validation (cf. Skinner, 1953, or Lundberg, 1939).[1] Another group within the positivistic camp, representing a softer line, recognizes some importance in subjective understanding for the development of a social science, but this importance is seen as largely heuristic (research generating) and rather as a part of the context of scientific discovery than that of scientific validation (cf. Rudner, 1966, and Abel in this volume). That is, such subjective understanding cannot confirm an hypothesis about the external world, but it can be useful in generating hypotheses subject to empirical test. This second position represents a much softer attitude towards the role of *verstehen* in that it allows it into the scientific arena - albeit in a very weak position.

On the side of those arguing for a distinctive social science, numerous positions can be found. At the extreme end are the hard-line humanists who argue the impossibility that social science will ever develop the kinds of law-like generalization found within the natural sciences. This argument often includes claims of indeterminacy within the social world (see Kuhn, 1964). This position argues that the sorts of covering-laws of explanation present in the physical sciences are impossible in principle for the social sciences and that subjective understanding must therefore be the proper goal for the student of things sociocultural (see Louch, 1966).

A far less extreme position can be found among those soft-line humanists who argue merely that a naturalistic approach (which they see as necessarily behavioristic) can be fruitful but only to a very limited degree (e.g., Sorokin 1928). Since most of man's activity is mediated by symbols, any system of behavioristic laws which sought to explain such actions could not ignore such ubiquitous sets of variables. Thus a social science patterned too strictly after the natural sciences would be highly limited (to the degree that it was possible at all), and, as such, it would be rather uninteresting. From this standpoint both naturalistic (covering-law) forms of explanation and *verstehen* should be sought.

Though these two positions are the most common within the antipositivistic camp, they are hardly exhaustive and numerous other varieties can be found represented among those writing today. The dispute over the proper role of subjective states has been present in some form throughout the social sciences. This brief collection, however, will concentrate upon the debate within sociology. Although some attention will be given to the highly related issues surrounding the role of *verstehen* as discussed in history, in the philosophy of science, and in psychology, the limits both of space and of the editor's competence in those disciplines necessitates leaving these most relevant debates for another volume. The student, however, should find ample leads into that literature through the brief references in our text and through the bibliographic entries at the end of this collection.

An outline of the history of this debate can be obtained through the introductory comments preceding the essays collected in this volume. As the reader will see, it is somewhat unfortunate that many of the disputes (at least among the social scientists) have been concerned less with the major issues at hand than with paying undue attention to exactly what a certain thinker (usually Max Weber) really meant in some classic earlier statement about *verstehen*. This has, I think, somewhat obscured the real issues. I would contend that the major questions to which the student of this debate should give his primary attention are:

1. Aside from the question of whether or not a social science patterned after the natural sciences can be established, should the goal of explanation in the natural sciences set the limits for explanation sought in the social sciences? In a sense this is to ask the

question: Even if we didn't need *verstehen* to build our science, would we want to add it?

2.   Are covering-laws of the sort found in the natural sciences impossible to obtain for the social sphere? And if they are possible, how limited or successful would such explanations be in accounting for most of the social action we seek to fully comprehend?

3.   To what degree is *verstehen* capable of scientific validation? That is, how good is it whan you have it at its best?

4.   To what degree is *verstehen* heuristic? Is it not possible that one's conviction of having *verstehen* might be more likely to keep someone from seeking other (external) forms of validation? And to what extent is *verstehen* likely to be misleading through its couching events in terms of everyday folk-categories rather than in terms of abstract, analytic dimensions (variables) that ultimately might prove more truly explanatory?

5.   To what degree is *verstehen* important in the validation process itself? Can one's *verstehen* confirm, supplement, or contradict what is otherwise validated?

6.   At what level of analysis is *verstehen* being sought? Is *verstehen* meant to indicate the individual motivations of social actors, or are we speaking here of group or cultural meanings shared by many actors and which merely provide a context for the motives of individual actors? And are we concerned with developing a meaningful picture of social reality in the mind of the social scientist, or simply in reconstructing the cognitive systems of the subjects (actors) under examination? If we seek the latter, is not all sociology forced to become social psychology? Is this not a move towards psychological reductionism and what has been called "methodological individualism"?

These questions certainly cannot be answered adequately here, but they represent some of the core issues in this ongoing dialogue.

Finally, a word might be said about the omissions in this collection. The limitations of space have forced the inclusion of only those selections which I thought might present the student with the core of this debate. Many important papers have necessarily been excluded. At one extreme, the writings of the positivistic

theorists like Lundberg (1939) and Catton (1966) which argue
for the most complete rejection of *verstehen* are not included.
Another extreme, represented by those who argue not only for
verstehen but for the position that only those active in a social
situation can properly analyze it - an argument well examined in
a recent paper by Merton (1972) dealing with the "insider" -
also were excluded. Special mention too, might be made of the
recent work by Bateson (1967) relating the *verstehen* issue to
cybernetic explanation, and Wilson's (1970) work on conceptions of interaction and sociological explanation. I can only hope
that the articles I have selected will tempt the student to examine
these and the other articles listed in the bibliography at the end of
this volume.

NOTE

1.   The full bibliographic citation corresponding to these short
references can be found in the bibliography at the end of this
volume.

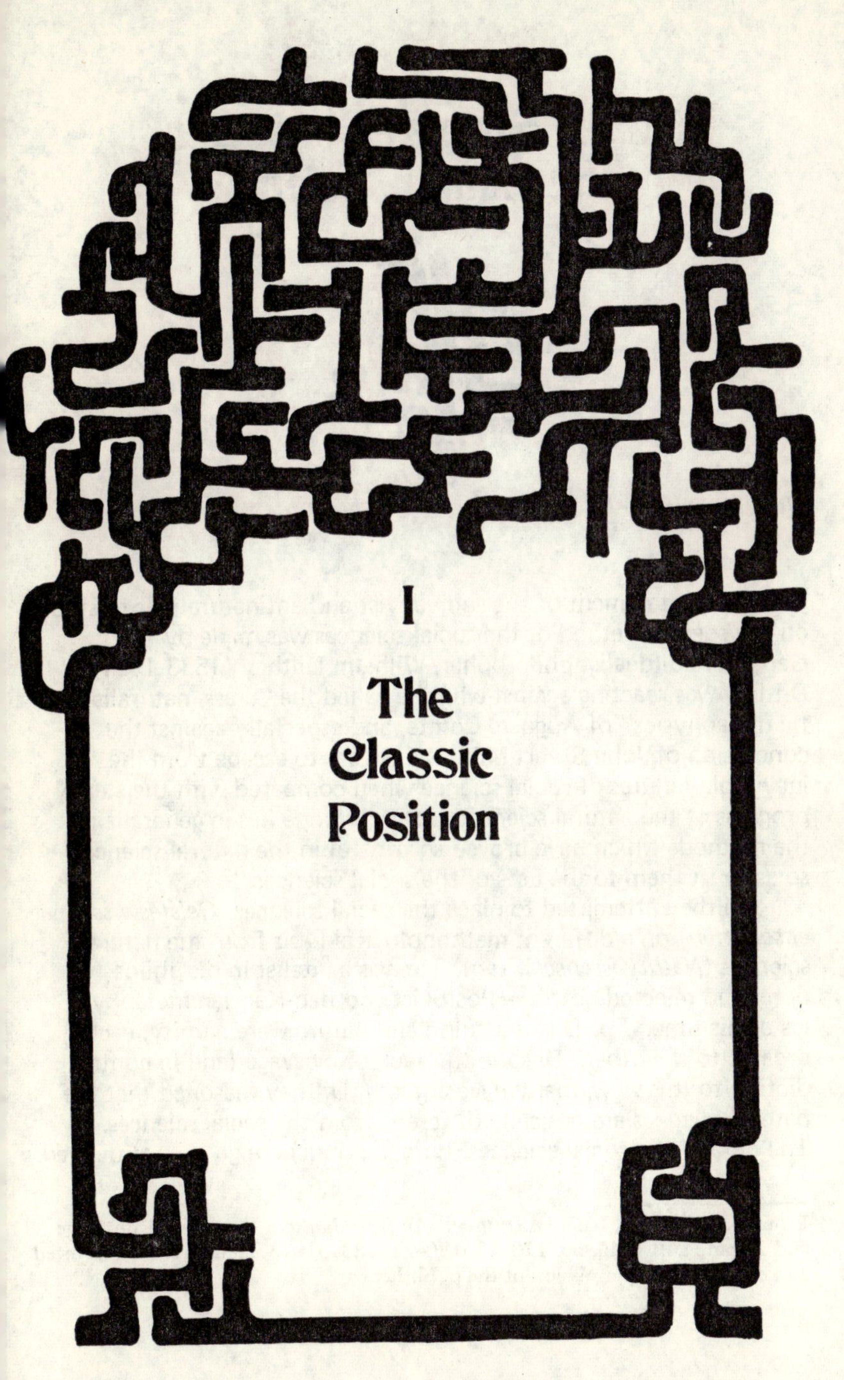

I

The
Classic
Position

1

On the Special Character of the Human Sciences

Wilhelm Dilthey

The classic statement of the subjectivist and antinaturalistic position on the special method of the social sciences was made by the German neo-Idealist philosopher, Wilhelm Dilthey (1833-1911).[1] Dilthey was reacting against what he called the "crass, naturalistic metaphysics" of Auguste Comte, and especially against the conclusion of John Stuart Mill: "If we are to escape from the inevitable failures of social science when compared with the steady progress of the natural sciences, our only hope lies in generalizing the methods which have proved so fruitful in the natural sciences so as to fit them to the uses of the social sciences."[2]

Dilthey attempted to place the social sciences (*Geisteswissenschaften*) on a different methodological basis from the natural sciences (*Naturwissenschaften*). He was a vitalist in his philosophy and rejected both the Positivist and neo-Kantian metaphysics of his time. For Dilthey, mind and nature were a unity, each organic to the other. Despite this lack of cleavage (and in contradiction to this view, many have argued), Dilthey reasoned that the natural sciences are basically different from the social sciences. The data of the social sciences (human minds) are given, not derived.

From H. A. Hodges, *Wilhelm Dilthey: An Introduction.* London: Routledge and Kegan Paul, 1944, pp. 110–13, 120–24, 128–31, 133 and 141–3. Reprinted and excerpted by permission of the publisher.

It is within himself that the social scientist is to find the key to the social world.

The natural sciences seek abstracted explanatory ultimates whereas the social sciences seek immediate understanding through insight into their raw data. Humanistic and artistic insights are the goals of the social sciences, and these are achieved not through the methods of the natural sciences but only by means of empathetic identification with the values and meanings examined in the minds of social actors. This is the process of subjective understanding or interpretation (*verstehen*), and we achieve such understanding through a process of "reliving" social events.

The *Geistwissenchaften* envisaged by Dilthey were to assert three types of propositions: (1) individual historical truths, (2) uniformities arrived at by abstract generalization, and (3) value judgements. Only the second of these goals is universally accepted by modern sociologists.

Since Dilthey saw *verstehen* as the central method of the social sciences, it is necessary to be selective in the examination of social life. This selection is made in terms of meaningful social types ultimately based on a psychic unity of mankind which allows the understanding of the past and unknown in terms of the present and known. In a never ending task, we must gradually understand this "ideal human type" in all its psychic variations through a constant rediscovery of the "I" in the "thou."

—MT

NOTES

1. For the writings of Dilthey in English see Rickman (1961) and Hodges (1944 and 1952). For writings on Dilthey's views see Becker and Barnes (1961) pp. 884-6, Holborn (1950), House (1936) pp. 393-6, Goldenweiser (1940) pp. 93-8, Masur (1952), and Rickman (1960).

2. *Logic*, II, Book VI, i.

On the Historical Background of Dilthey's Work. At the close of the Middle Ages the emancipation of the special sciences began. . . . but hitherto the historical school has not broken through the inner limitations which were bound to hinder its theoretical development and its influence on life. Its study and evaluation of historical phenomena was not brought into relation with the analysis of the facts of consciousness, and so was not based upon what is in the last resort the only secure knowledge; in short, it had no philosophical foundation. It had no healthy relationship with epistemology and psychology. For that reason it also failed to develop an explanatory method: and yet historical contemplation and comparative methods by themselves can neither erect an independent system of the human studies nor obtain influence upon life. So it was that, when Comte, J. S. Mill, and Buckle renewed the attempt to solve the riddle of the historical world by a transference of principles and methods from natural science, the deeper and more vital outlook, which had neither firm foundations nor the power to explicate itself, could make only an ineffective protest against the inferior and more poverty-stricken outlook, which had command of analysis. . . .

The answers given to these questions by Comte and the positivists, J. S. Mill and the empiricists, seemed to me to mutilate historical reality in order to adapt it to the ideas and methods of the natural sciences. The reaction against this, brilliantly represented by Lotze's *Mikrokosmos*, seemed to me to sacrifice the justified independence of the special sciences, the fruitful power of their empirical methods, and the security of their foundations, in the interests of a sentimental frame of mind, a wistful longing to recall the vanished days when knowledge was a way to the satisfaction of the heart. Nowhere but in inner experience, in the facts of consciousness, did I find a firm anchorage for my thought, and I venture to believe that no reader will be able to escape the force of my argument on this point. All knowledge is knowledge of experience ; but the original unity of all experience and its resulting validity are conditioned by the factors which mould the consciousness within which it arises, i.e., by the whole of our nature. This standpoint, which consistently realizes the impossibility of going behind these conditions, of seeing as it were without an eye or directing the gaze of knowledge behind the eye itself, I call the epistemological standpoint; modern knowledge can recognize no other. But then it further became apparent to me that from this standpoint the independence of the human studies finds a foundation

such as the historical school required. For from this standpoint
our view of the whole natural world turns out to be a mere shadow
cast by a reality hidden from us, while it is only in the facts of consciousness given in inner experience that we possess reality as it is.
The analysis of these facts lies at the center of the human studies,
and so, in accord with the standpoint of the historical school, in
knowing the principles which govern the world of mind we remain
within that world, and the human studies form an independent
system by themselves.

• • •

On the Higher Forms of Understanding. The secret of the person
invites us of its own accord to ever new and deeper attempts to
understand. And in such understanding there is opened up the
realm of individuals which embraces human beings and their creations. Herein lies the most characteristic service rendered by understanding to the human studies. Objective mind and the power
of the individual together determine the world of mind. History
rests on the understanding of both.

• • •

The position which the higher type of understanding takes
up in face of its object is determined by its task, which is to discover a living unity in the given. This is only possible if the systematic unity which subsists in the subject's own lived experience, and
is experienced in innumerable instances, is always present and
available with all its inherent possibilities. This state of things,
which is involved in the task of understanding, we call a projection
of the self into a person or a work. . . .

This active presence of the mental system privately enjoyed,
which follows from the very terms in which the problem of understanding is set, is also called the *transference* of the subject's own
self into a given complex of expressions.

On the basis of this projection, this transposition, arises the
highest form in which the totality of mental life can operate in
understanding —that of reproducing or reliving (*das Nachbilden
oder Nacherleben*). In the operation of understanding as such the
direction of the life-process itself is reversed. But a perfect sharing
of life is only possible if our understanding moves forward along
the actual line of events. Constantly striding forward, it advances

with the life-process itself. In this way the process of self-projec-
tion or transposition widens out. Reliving means creating along
the line of events. Thus we go forward with history, with an event
in a far land or with something that is going on in the soul of a
human being close to us. It reaches its fulfillment where the event
has passed through the consciousness of the poet, the artist, or the
historian, and now lies before us fixed and enduring in his work.

Thus a lyrical poem enables us by the sequence of its lines
to relive a connected mass of lived experience: not the actual experience which stimulated the poet, but that which, on the basis
of it, the poet puts into the mouth of an ideal person. The sequence of scenes in a play enables us to relive segments of the lives
of the persons represented. The narrative of the novelist or the
historian, which follows the historical process, produces in us a reliving of that process. It is the triumph of reliving that, in it, the
fragments of a process are so filled out that we think we have a
continuous whole before us.

But wherein does this reliving consist? The process interests
us here only from the point of view of its function; we do not pro-
pose to give a psychological explanation of it. Thus we shall not
go into the relation between this conception and that of sympathy
or that of empathy, although the connection between them is evident from the fact that sympathy heightens the energy with which
we relive. Let us turn our attention to the significant function of
this reliving as a contribution to the process of making the world
of mind our own. It rests on two elements. Every vivid imaginative presentment of a milieu and an outward situation stimulates
a reliving process in us. And fancy can strengthen or weaken the
emphasis upon the attitudes, forces, feelings, strivings, lines of
thought which are contained in our own lives, and in this way can
reproduce any other person's mental life. The curtain rises.
Richard appears, and a lively mind, following his words, mien, and
movements, can relive something which lies outside any possibility of his real actual life. The fantastic forest in *As You Like It*
puts us in a mood to reproduce any eccentricity.

And in this reliving lies an important part of the gain of mental treasure which we owe to the historian and the poet. The life-
process brings about in every man a continual determination by
which the possibilities inherent in him come to be limited. The

crystallization of his nature constantly determines his further development. In short, whether he contemplates the fixity of his circumstances or the form of his acquired experience, he always finds that the circle of new perspectives upon life and inner changes of his personal character is a limited one. But understanding opens to him a wide realm of possibilities which are not to hand in the determination of his actual life. For me, as for most people today, the possibility of living through religious experiences in my own person is narrowly circumscribed. But when I run through Luther's letters and writings, the accounts given by his contemporaries, the records of the religious conferences and councils and of his official activities, I live through a religious process of such eruptive power, of such energy, in which the stake is life or death, that it lies beyond any possibility of personal experience for a man of our day. But I can relive it. I project myself into the circumstances: everything in them strains towards such an extraordinary development of the life of the religious mind. I see in the monasteries a technique of intercourse with the invisible world, giving to monkish souls an eye constantly directed towards the things of another world. Here theological controversies become questions of inner experience. I see how that which thus takes shape in the monasteries spreads through innumerable channels—pulpits, confessionals, professorial chairs, writings—into the lay world; and then I observe how councils and religious movements have spread everywhere the doctrine of the invisible Church and universal priesthood, and how it enters into relation with the liberation of personality in secular life; how in this way what had been achieved in the solitude of the cell, in struggles of such violence as has been described, maintains itself in face of the Church. Christianity as a power to shape life even in the family, in men's vocations, in political relationships—that is a new force confronting the spirit of the time in the towns and everywhere where higher work is done, in Hans Sachs, in Dürer. When Luther goes his way at the head of this movement, we live through his development on the basis of a relationship which extends from human nature in general to the religious sphere, and from that through its historical determinations to his individuality. And so this process opens up to us a religious world in him and his contemporaries of the early Reformation, which widens our horizon to include possibil-

ities of human life which are accessible to us only in this way.
Thus man, determined from within, can live in imagination through
many other existences. Before man limited by circumstances
there open out strange beauties in the world, and tracts of life
which he can never reach. To generalize—man, bound and determined by the reality of life, is set free not only by art—as has often been shown—but also through the understanding of history.
And this effect of history, which its most recent detractors have
not seen, is broadened and deepened on the wider levels of the
historical consciousness.

• • •

On the Intuitive Element in Understanding. By virtue of these relationships *scientific exegisis* or *interpretation*, i.e., understanding
by *skilled* reproduction, has always an element of genius, i.e., it
reaches a high degree of perfection only through inner affinity and
sympathy. Thus the works of the ancients began to be fully understood again in the Renaissance period, when similar conditions
had for their consequence an affinity between the men of the two
ages. This inner relationship, which makes transposition possible,
is therefore the presupposition of all hermeneutic rules, and it is
only by a methodical procedure resting on this living relationship
that they can deduce their particular results in dealing with various
objects. It is the same living relationship too, in the first instance,
which enables us to amplify tradition and exclude what is not
authentic, whatever rational factors may also contribute. There
is no scientific process which could leave this living reproduction
behind as a subordinate element. Here is the mother earth from
which even the most abstract operations in the human studies
must continually draw their strength. Understanding here can
never be transmuted into rational comprehension. It is vain
to wish to make the hero or the genius comprehensible in terms
of miscellaneous circumstances. The most proper approach to him
is the most subjective. For the highest possibility of grasping what
is powerful in him lies in the lived experience of his effects upon
ourselves, in the enduring conditions to which our own life is subjected because of him. Ranke's Luther, Goethe's Winkelmann, the
Pericles of Thucydides proceeded from this kind of relation to the
living power of a hero.

• • •

On the Psychological Foundation of Human Studies. An empiricism which renounces the attempt to ground what happens in the mind on an understanding of the system of mental life is necessarily sterile. This can be shown in each several one of the human studies. Each of them needs psychological knowledge. . . . It is so, and no building of barriers between departments can alter it: as the cultural systems, economic life, law, religion, art, and science, and the outer organization of societies in associations like the family, community, Church, and State, have arisen from the living system of the human mind, so in the end they can only be understood in terms of it. Psychical facts form the most important element in them, therefore without psychical analysis they cannot be made transparent. They contain system in themselves because mental life is a system. Thus the understanding of this inner system in us everywhere conditions the knowledge of them.

• • •

We know natural objects from without through our senses. However we may break them up or divide them, we never reach their ultimate elements in this way. We supply such elements by an amplification of experience. Again, the senses, regarded from the point of view of their purely physiological function, never give us the unity of the object. This exists for us only through a synthesis of the sense-stimuli which arises from within. This statement would remain correct even if the analysis of unitary perception into sensations and their syntheses were regarded only as a heuristic device. And when we place objects in the relations of cause and effect, for this too the sensory impressions contain only the condition, which lies in regular succession, whereas the causal relation itself again arises through a synthesis which springs from within us. This statement also holds good whether we make this synthesis come from the understanding, or whether, as I explained in an earlier essay, the relation of cause and effect is only a derivative of the living experience of the will subjected to the pressure of another, so that the basis of this relation is a primary and constitutive element in experience, and it is only afterwards that the living relation is interpreted intellectually by abstract thought. Thus, however, we may conceive the origin of our representations of objects and their causal relations, in any case the sensory stimuli, their coexistence and succession, include no part of the connection which lies in the objects and their causal relations.

How different is the way in which mental life is given to us! In contrast to external perception, inner perception rests upon an awareness (*Innewerden*), a lived experience (*Erleben*), it is immediately given. Here, in sensation or in the feeling of pleasure accompanying it, something simple and indivisible is given to us. No matter how the sensation of a violet colour may have arisen, considered as an inner phenomenon it is something indivisible. If we perform an act of thought, a distinguishable plurality of inner facts is held together in it in the indivisible unity of a function, and thus there arises in inner experience something new, which has no analogy in nature.

• • •

On the Peculiar Nature of the Human Studies. We can now mark off the human studies from the natural sciences by quite clear criteria. These lie in the attitude of mind described above, by which, in contrast with natural-scientific knowledge, the object of the human studies is constituted. Mankind, if apprehended only by perception and perceptual knowledge, would be for us a physical fact, and as such it would be accessible only to natural-scientific knowledge. It becomes an object for the human studies only in so far as human states are consciously lived, in so far as they find expression in living utterances, and in so far as these expressions are understood. Of course this relationship of life, expression, and understanding embraces not only the gestures, looks, and words in which men communicate, or the enduring mental creations in which the depths of the creator's mind open themselves to the spectator, or the permanent objectifications of mind in social structures, through which the common background of human nature shines and is permanently visible and certain to us. The mind-body unit of life is known to itself through the same double relationship of lived experience and understanding, it is aware of itself in the present, it rediscovers itself in memory as something that once was; but when it tries to hold fast and to apprehend its states, when it turns its attention upon itself, the narrow limits of such an introspective method of self-knowledge make themselves felt. Only from his actions, his fixed utterances, his effects upon others, can man learn about himself; thus he learns to know himself only by the roundabout way of understanding. What we once were, how we developed and became what we are, we learn from the way in which we acted, the plans which we once adopted, the way in which we made ourselves felt in our vocation, from old dead letters, from judgments on us which were spoken long ago. In short, it is through the process of understanding that life in its depths is made clear to itself, and on the other hand we understand ourselves and others only when we transfer our own lived experience into every kind of expression of our own and other people's life. Thus everywhere the relation between lived experience, expression, and understanding is the proper procedure by which mankind as an object in the human studies exists for us. The human studies are thus founded on this relation between lived experience, expression, and understanding. Here for the first time we reach a quite clear criterion by which the delimitation of the human studies can be definitively carried out. A study belongs to the human studies only if its object becomes accessible to us through the attitude which is founded on the relation between life, expression, and understanding.

From this common nature of the studies in question follow all the peculiarities which have been emphasized in discussions on the human studies, or cultural studies, or history, as constituting their nature. Thus the peculiar relation in which the unique, singular individual stands here to universal regularities. Then the combination which takes place here of statements of fact, judgments of value, and ideas of purpose. Again, "the apprehension of the singular or individual is in them as much an ultimate end as is the development of abstract uniformities." But still more will result from this; all the leading concepts with which this group of studies operates are different from the corresponding ones in the field of natural science.

2

On Subjective Interpretation
in the Social Sciences

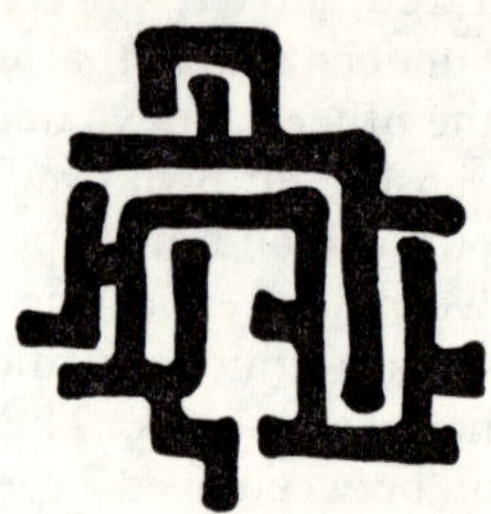

Max Weber

Following the attack of Dilthey on the positivistic position, the Neo-Idealist position was probably best carried forward by his student, Eduard Spranger (1882 - 1963), who extended Dilthey's argument and method (with Hegelian overtones) into psychology and personality theory.[1] Contemporary with Dilthey's arguments, however, the Neo-Kantian philosopher Heinrich Rickert (1863 - 1936), following the earlier work of the philosopher Wilhelm Windelband (1848 - 1915), attacked from another direction.[2] Rickert disagreed with Dilthey's distinction between the social and the natural sciences. He argued that the major difference between the social and natural sciences was not in their empirical reality (the way in which they are apprehended) but in the unique character of historical events in contrast to the general character of natural events. Thus the social scientist must study the individual and unique (*ideographic*) event whereas the natural scientist studies the general and repetitive (*nomothetic*) events. According to Rickert, the social sciences must relinquish any search for historical laws. Rickert also argued against Dilthey's position that the social sciences should establish judgments of social policy and values.

From Max Weber (trans. by H. P. Secher), *Basic Concepts in Sociology*. New York: The Citadel Press, 1962, pp. 29-51. Reprinted by permission of the publisher.

Despite Rickert's disagreements with Dilthey, he did argue strongly for the necessity of subjective understanding for the social sciences. Rickert contended that we have to know the values and goals of social actors in order to fully explain their behaviors. Rickert expressly dissents from the use of the term *verstehen*; but the method he developed, with its emphasis on the meaning of things (*Sinn*) to social actors as necessary for the understanding of social phenomena, clearly places him in the school of *verstehende soziologie* which was to be more fully elaborated by Max Weber and Werner Sombart.

Combining the influences of both Dilthey and Rickert, but bringing the German Idealistic and Kantian doctrines into a closer relationship with the positivistic emphasis on causes, empirical verification, and generalization (the search for laws), Max Weber (1864 - 1920) stated his most influential defense of the *verstehen* position.[3] Although others, especially the economist Werner Sombart (1863 – 1941),[4] gave important defenses of the position, it is clearly Weber's presentation that has been most influential and most cited (particularly within sociology).

In the following statement of his position, Weber argues for the importance and necessity of subjective understanding for the development of sociology — but only as a *first step* in the process of the search for social causes. *Verstehen* then is seen as a *necessary* but not *sufficient* condition for the development of explanation within the social sciences

—MT

NOTES

1.   Spranger's chief work, *Die Lebensformen* (1914), was translated by J. W. Pigors as *Types of Man* (1928). For a good brief survey of Spranger's contributions, see Loemker (1967).

2.   Rickert's major work in this area is the still untranslated *Die Grenzen der naturwissenschaftlichen Beriffsbildung* (1902), but he presented a concise treatment in his *Kulturwissenschaft und Naturwissenschaft* (1899). For excellent short treatments of Rickert's contributions, see Anchor (1967) and Goldenweiser (1940).

3.   A different translation of the same passage by Weber reproduced in this volume can be found in the translation by Henderson and Parsons (see Weber, 1947). For further elaboration by Weber on the verstehen

question, see his essays translated by Shils and Finch (see Weber, 1949). For an excellent brief statement of Weber's contributions and a full bibliography of the major works dealing with him, see Bendix (1968).

4.   Sombart's main work dealing with this issue is *Die drei National-ökonomien* (1929). For works dealing with Sombart's general contributions to the verstehen issue, see House (1936), Becker and Barnes (1961), and, especially, Kuczynski (1968), which includes extensive bibliography. For a brief but relevant work in English, see Sombart (1949).

The term "sociology" is open to many different interpretations. In the context used here it shall mean that science which aims at the interpretative understanding of social behavior in order to gain an explanation of its causes, its course, and its effects. It will be called human "behavior" only in so far as the person or persons involved engage in some subjectively meaningful action. Such behavior may be mental or external; it may consist in action or omission to act. The term "social behavior" will be reserved for activities whose intent is related by the individuals involved to the conduct of others and is oriented accordingly.

A. METHODOLOGICAL FOUNDATIONS

1.   "Meaning" is used here in two different senses. First, there is actual conduct by a specific actor in a given historical situation or the rough approximation based on a given quantity of cases involving many actors; and, second, there is the conceptually "ideal type" of subjective meaning attributed to a hypothetical actor in a given type of conduct. In neither sense can it be used as an objectively "valid" or as a metaphysically fathomable "true" meaning. Herein lies the distinction between the behavioral sciences, such as Sociology and History and the orthodox disciplines, such as Jurisprudence, Logic, Ethics, or Esthetics, whose purpose it is to determine the "true" and "valid" meaning of the objects of their analysis.

2.   The line between meaningful and merely responsive behavior (i.e., subjectively not meaningful) is extremely fluid. A significant part of all sociologically relevant behavior, principally purely traditional behavior (see below), fluctuates between the two. Meaning-

ful, i.e. subjectively·understandable conduct does not figure at all in many cases of psychophysical processes, or, if it does, is recognizable only by the expert; mystical experiences which cannot be adequately communicated in words are never fully understandable for anyone who is not susceptible to such experiences. On the other hand, the ability to perform a similar action is not a precondition to understanding; it is not necessary "to be Caesar in order to understand Caesar." To be able to put one's self in the place of the actor is important for clearness of understanding but not an absolute precondition for meaningful interpretation. Understandable and non-understandable parts of a process are often inextricably intertwined.

3. All interpretation, as does science generally, strives for clarity and verifiable proof. Such proof of understanding will be either of a rational, i.e., logical or mathematical, or of an emotionally emphatic, artistically appreciative, character. Rational proof can be supplied in the sphere of behavior by a clear intellectual grasp of everything within its intended context of meaning. Emphatic proof in the sphere of behavior will be supplied by complete sympathetic emotional participation. Direct and unambiguous intelligibility is rational understanding of the highest order, especially in mathematically and logically related propositions. We understand plainly what it means when anyone uses the proposition $2 + 2 = 4$, or the Pythagorean theorem in reasoning or argument, or when a chain of reasoning is logically executed in accordance with accepted ways of thought. In the same way we understand the actions of a person who tries to achieve a certain goal by choosing appropriate means, if the facts of the situation on the basis of which he makes his choice are familiar to us. Any interpretation of such rationally purposeful action possesses — for an understanding of the means employed — the highest degree of proof. Not with the same accuracy, but still accurate enough for most purposes of explanation, it is possible to understand errors (including problem entanglements) to which we ourselves are susceptible or whose origin can be detected by sympathetic self-analysis. On the other hand, many ultimate *goals* or *values* toward which experience shows that human behavior may be oriented often cannot be understood as such, though it is possible to grasp them intellectually. The more radically they vary from our own ultimate values, the more difficult it is for us to understand them through sympathetic participa-

tion. Depending upon the circumstances of a particular case, it must then suffice to achieve only a purely intellectual understanding of such values or, failing that, a simple acceptance of them as given data. As far as is possible, the conduct motivated by these values can then be understood on the basis of whatever opportunities appear to be available for a sympathetic emotional and/or intellectual interpretation at different stages of its development. Here belong many zealous acts of religion or piety which are quite incomprehensible to those not susceptible to such values; as well as the extreme rationalistic fanaticism typical of the exponents of the "rights of man" theories which are abhorrent to those who, for their part emphatically repudiate them.

As our susceptibility grows, the more readily are we able to experience such true passions as fear, anger, ambition, envy, jealousy love, enthusiasm, pride, vengeance, pity, devotion and other desires of every kind, as well as the irrational behavior issuing from them. Even when the degree of intensity in which these emotions are found far surpasses our own potentialities for experiential understanding, we can still interpret intellectually their impact on the direction taken by our behavior as well as the choice of means used to implement it. For purposes of systematic scientific analysis it will be convenient to represent all irrational, emotionally conditioned elements of conduct as deviations from a conceptually pure type of goal-oriented behavior. For example, an analysis of a crisis on the stock exchange would be most conveniently attempted in the following manner: First, a determination of how it would have run its course in the absence of irrational factors; second, using the foregoing as a hypothetical premise, the irrational components are then singled out as "deviation" from the norm. In the same way, the determination of the rational course of a political or military campaign needs first to be made in the light of all known circumstances and known goals of the participants. Only then will it be possible to account for the causal significance of irrational factors as deviations from the ideal type.

The construction of a purely rational "goal-oriented" course of conduct, because of its clear understandability and rational unambiguity, serves sociology as an "ideal type." Thus we are aided in our understanding of the way in which actual goal-oriented conduct is influenced by irrational factors of every kind (such as

emotion, errors) and which then can be classified as deviations
from the original hypothesized behavior.

Only in this respect and because of methodological efficiency
can the method of sociology be considered "rationalistic." Naturally, this procedure may not be interpreted as a rationalistic bias
on the part of sociology, but simply as a methodological device.
Neither can it be considered as evidence of the predominance of
rationalism in human existence. To what extent the reality of rationalism does determine conduct is not to be considered here.
That there is a danger of rationalistic interpretations in the wrong
place will not be denied. Unfortunately, all experience confirms
the existence of such a danger.

4. On the other hand, certain "meaningless" (i.e., devoid of subjective meaning) processes and phenomena exist in all sciences of
human behavior. They act as stimuli, or effects, and they either
encourage or inhibit human conduct. Such "meaningless" behavior
should not be confused with inanimate or non-human behavior.
Every artifact (e.g., a machine) acquires meaning only to the extent that its production and use will serve to influence human behavior; such meaning may be quite varied in its purposes. But without reference to such meaning the object remains completely unintelligible.

What makes this object intelligible then is its relation to human
behavior in its role of either means or end. It is this relationship of
which the individual can claim to have awareness and to which his
conduct has been oriented. Only in terms of such categories does
an understanding of objects of this kind arise.

On the other hand, all processes or conditions remain "meaningless" if they cannot be related to a meaningful purpose; this regardless of whether they are inanimate, human or inhuman. In other words, they are devoid of meaning if they cannot be related to
behavior in their role as means or ends, but operate simply as stimuli, either releasing or inhibiting such behavior.

It is possible, for example, to view the bursting of the River
Dollart in 1277 as a powerful stimulus to ensuing migratory movements. The process of decaying, indeed the whole organic life
cycle — from the helplessness of the infant to that of the old man
— obtains its primary sociological moment from the various ways
in which human behavior has become conditioned to these facts.

Certain psychic or psychophysical phenomena such as fatigue, discipline, and memory must be viewed as yet another category of facts that are devoid of meaning; also typical states of euphoria caused by certain conditions of self-punishment, or typical variations in reactions of individuals depending on time, precision, and nature. In the last analysis the principle to be adhered to is the same as with other unintelligible phenomena; they provide the source of "data" for both the observer and the participant.

It is altogether possible that in the future research may uncover non-intelligible uniformities under what had appeared to be, until then, distinctly meaningful behavior, though this has hardly been the case so far. For example, differences in inherited biological characteristics (racial) must be accepted by sociology in the same way as are the physiological facts of the need of nutrition or of the effects of senescence on human behavior. Such data would be acceptable only, of course, insofar as statistically conclusive proof could be supplied of their influence on sociologically relevant behavior. The recognition of such causal significance would not change in the least the task of sociology, which is to interpret intelligible human conduct. The result would be merely to introduce at certain points the same unintelligible data that are already present (see above) into the complex of meaningful motivations; such data as, for example, the typical relations existing between the frequency of certain goal-oriented behavior or the extent of its rationality and the cephalic index or skin color or any other physiological inherited characteristic.

5. Understanding may be of two kinds: first, direct empirical understanding of the meaning of a given act (incl. a verbal utterance). It is in this sense that we "understand" (i.e., directly) the meaning of the proposition that 2 x 2 = 4, when we hear or read it. Here we experience direct, rational understanding of an idea. In the same way, we understand a fit of anger as expressed by exclamations, facial expression or irrational movements. This is direct empirical understanding of irrational emotional reactions and it belongs in the same category as the observation of the action of a woodcutter or of somebody who reaches for a doorknob to shut the door or who aims a gun at an animal. This is rational empirical observation of behavior.

Understanding may also be of a second kind, and this is known as explanatory understanding. We are capable of understanding the motives of anyone who states that 2 x 2 = 4 (either orally or in writing) precisely at a particular time and under a definite set of circumstances. Such understanding may be gained if the person under observation is engaged in some bookkeeping task or in a scientific demonstration or some other project of which this task is an essential part. This is rationally based understanding of motivation, i.e., the act is seen as part of an intelligible situation. Motivational is added to observational understanding if we know that the aiming of the gun is done for recreation and the chopping of wood for compensation. Or, in the former instance, the act may be done in order to release certain pent-up emotions, in which case the conduct assumes an irrational character, or because the person aiming the gun has been ordered to do so as a member of a firing squad, or he is firing at an enemy (in either case his behavior is again rational) or because he is exercising his desire for revenge (in which case he reverts to irrational behavior). Finally, we understand motivationally a fit of anger, if we know that its immediate cause can be found in jealousy, hurt pride or injured vanity, all of which are emotionally caused and therefore traceable to irrational motives.

In all the above situations the behavior in question can be designated as part of an understandable sequence of emotions. Such understanding can be accepted as true explanation of the actual course of behavior. For a science dealing with the true meaning of behavior, explanation requires: a grasp of the context of meaning within which the actual course of action occurs. In all such cases, even those involving emotional processes, the subjective meaning within the relevant context of its meaning will be designated "intended" meaning; thus we move beyond the customary usage which regards as intentional only (rationally-purposive) goal-oriented behavior.

6.   To understand means therefore in all these cases: interpretative understanding of *a.*) concrete individual cases, as for example in historical analysis; *b.*) average cases, that is, approximate estimates, as in sociological mass analysis; or *c.*) a pure type of a frequently occurring scientifically formulated construct. Such ideally typical constructs are, for example, the concepts and ax-

ioms of pure economic theory. They show how a given type of human behavior would occur, on a strictly rational basis, unaffected by errors or emotional factors, and if, further, it were directed only to a single goal. Actual behavior takes this course only rarely (e.g., on the stock exchange) and then only approximately so as to correspond to the ideal type. (On the purpose of such constructions, see my discussions in *Archiv f. Sozialwissenschaft* vol. XIX, p. 64ff [Reprinted in *Ges. Aufs. z. Wissenschaftslehre,* p. 190ff] and below, sec. 11.)

To be sure, every interpretation strives to achieve utmost verifiability. But even the most verifiable interpretation cannot claim the character of being causally valid. It will remain only a particularly plausible hypothesis. Thus what appears to be conscious motivation to the individual involved may only serve to hide the deeper lying motives and repressions that are really at the root of his behavior and in this way invalidating even the most sincere attempts at self-analysis. In such a case it becomes the task of sociology to inquire into the deeper meaning of such motivation and interpret it accurately, even though this motivation has not been fully part of the conscious behavior of the individual in question: it becomes therefore a borderline case of meaningful interpretation.

Again, forms of behavior which appear to the observer to share the same or similar characteristics may be based on a variety of motives on the part of the individual actor. Situations of this kind which appear to share some superficial characteristics must be interpreted quite differently, even if this leads to conflicting analysis. Finally, the individuals involved in any given situation frequently respond to opposing impulses, all of which can be understood by us. We know from experience it is not always possible to estimate even approximately the relative strength of motives and very often we cannot even be certain of our own interpretation. Only the final result of the conflict provides us with a solid basis for judgment. The verification of interpretation by its results, i.e., the decisiveness of the actual course of events, is, as is true of all hypotheses, indispensable. Unfortunately, such verifiable interpretations can be obtained with relative accuracy only in a very few and special cases of the kind suitable for psychological experimentation; or, aiming at a different degree of approximation, through statistically quantifiable data of mass phenomena. For the rest, there remains only the possibility of comparing a maximum number of historical processes or routine phenomena of everyday experience and of similar appearance but differing substantially regarding the motivational factor under investigation. This is the fundamental task of comparative sociology. Unfortunately, there often remains only the uncertain instrument of purely hypothetical experiments, which ignores certain elements in the chain of motivation and leads instead to the construction of a merely probable course of events that might lend itself to causal attribution.

For example, the postulate known as Gresham's Law is a rational interpretation of human conduct within a given context and on the basis of an ideal hypothesis of a purely rational course. To what extent such behavior really follows Gresham's Law can be ascertained only on the basis of statistical information concerning the disappearance of under-valued money, and generally our experience has shown the validity of this law. In this case the data were first accumulated, followed by the formulation of a suitable generalization. But without such a successful interpretation we could not have satisfied our need for true causal understanding. On the other hand, the absence of proof that the action inferred from this behavior occurs with some regularity, would make a law, no matter how much theoretical proof could be obtained, quite valueless for purposes of concrete analysis. In this case the theoretical interpretation of motivation and its empirical verification display considerable conformity and there are a sufficient number of cases to consider proof to have been established satisfactorily.

But to use another illustration, the ingenious theory developed by Eduard Meyers as to the causal significance of the battles of Salamis and Platea for the unique evolution of Greek and hence occidental culture generally (He bases it on symptomatic facts concerning the attitude of the Hellenic oracles and of the prophets toward the Persians) does not submit easily to such proof. Verification can be obtained only by reference to the conduct of the Persians in cases where they were victorious, as for example in Jerusalem, Egypt, and Asia Minor, and even this verification must necessarily remain incomplete in many respects. What provides this hypothesis with such strong support is its striking rational plausibility. Yet in many cases of such highly plausible historical interpretations, what is lacking is the possibility of the kind of proof that was still feasible even in this case. Under such circumstances the interpretation must remain purely hypothetical.

7. "Motivation" as used here refers to a complex of meaning which appears to the individual involved or to the observer to be sufficient reason for his conduct. A *meaningfully adequate level* of understanding refers to a subjective interpretation of a coherent course of behavior whose component parts articulate with each other, within the context of our accustomed modes of thought and feeling, to the point of constituting a "typical"complex of meaning. It is usually called "correct," rather than typical. In contrast, we will consider an interpretation of a sequence of events to be *causally adequate*, if on the basis of past experience it appears probable that it will always occur in the same way.

An example of a meaningfully adequate level of interpretation can be encountered in the correct solution of an arithmetical problem, if it accords with accepted norms of calculation and of reasoning. On the other hand, a causally adequate interpretation of the same phenomenon would concern the statistical probability that, in line with tested empirical generalizations, there would be a correct or incorrect solution of the same problem. Though this would accept prevailing normative standards it would also take into account typical errors or confusions. Causal explanations therefore postulate: a rarely quantifiable but always somehow calculable probability that any certain observable overt or subjective event is either followed or accompanied by another event.

A correct causal interpretation of a concrete course of behavior is achieved when such overt behavior and its motives have both been correctly ascertained and if, at the same time, their relationship has become intelligible in a meaningful way. A correct causal interpretation of a typical course of behavior then can be taken to mean that the process which is claimed to be typical is shown to lend itself to both meaningful and causally adequate interpretation. If no meaning attaches itself to such typical behavior, then regardless of the degree of uniformity or the statistical preciseness of probability, it still remains an incomprehensible statistical probability, whether it deals with an overt or subjective process. On the other hand, even the most perfectly adequate meaning is causally significant from a sociological point of view only if we have proof that in all likelihood the conduct in question normally unfolds in a meaningful way. In order for this to occur there must be determinable some degree of frequency of approximation to an average or an ideal type.

In the present context, statistical uniformities constitute intelligible types of behavior, i.e., sociological generalizations, only when they manifest the understandable subjective meaning of a course of social behavior. Again, only those rational constructs of subjectively intelligible conduct can be considered as sociological types of empirical process if they can be empirically observed with at least a degree of approximation. It is hardly ever the case that the actual likelihood of the occurrence of a given course of behavior will always be directly proportional to the clarity of subjective interpretation. At any rate, only experience can tell whether this will always be true. It is possible, after all, to obtain statistical information of processes that are devoid of meaning as well as those with meaning: the amount of rainfall, the death rate, phenomena of fatigue, and the productivity of machines are good examples of the former, while crime rates, occupational distributions, price statistics, and crop acreage statistics are examples of the latter; and only in these latter examples is it possible to speak of sociological statistics. Of course there are many cases, as in crop statistics, which contain both kinds of meaning.

8. Processes and uniformities which because of their unintelligibility are not designated here as sociological phenomena or uniformities are not necessarily less important on that account. This is true also for sociology in our present context, which implies a restriction to subjectively understandable phenomena and which no one is forced to accept. They are simply moved into a different category from that of meaningful behavior, which is methodologically unavoidable: thus they become conditions, stimuli, inhibiting or encouraging the environment in which behavior occurs.

9. "Behavior" in the sense of subjectively intelligible orientation of behavior exists only as the behavior of one or more individual persons. For other analytical purposes it may be useful and even necessary to look at the individual as a collection of cells or a bundle of biochemical reactions, or conceive of his psyche as composed of a number of variously defined elements. This would

certainly yield valuable insight into causal relationships. Yet we
do not really understand subjectively the behavior of these elements as expressed in these uniformities. We do not even understand it with psychic elements: the more scientifically exact their
definition, the less do we understand them; this never leads to interpretation in terms of subjective meaning. But for both sociology
and history the real object for analysis should be the deeper meaning of certain behavior. The behavior of certain physiological en-
tities, e.g., cells, or of any sort of psychic elements, may at least
be observed in principle in such a way as to lead to the creation of
certain postulates applicable to individually uniform phenomena.
But the subjective understanding of behavior recognizes such facts
and uniformities as well as any others not capable of subjective interpretation: for example, of physical, astronomical, geological,
meteorological, geographical, botanical, zoological, anatomical
data as well as of such data relating to psychopathology which are
devoid of subjective meaning or those of the scientific conditions
giving rise to technological progress.

For still other purposes of analyses, e.g., legal or practical ends,
it may be convenient and even unavoidable to treat social groups,
such as the state, cooperative associations, business corporations,
and foundations as if they were individual persons with rights and
duties and as the executors of legally significant conduct. But for
sociologically meaningful interpretations such organizations are
merely the result of distinct behavior of individual persons, since
they alone can engage as agents in any kind of meaningful behavior.
Nevertheless, the sociologist for his purposes can hardly ignore such
concepts of collectivity that derive from different vantage points
because the subjective interpretation of behavior is related to such
concepts in at least three different ways.

a.)   Such interpretation is frequently forced to work with similar
(even identical) concepts in order to establish a meaningful terminology generally. Both legal as well as lay terminology defines the
state as a legal concept and a phenomenon of social behavior to
which its legal rules are relevant. But for sociological purposes the
term "state" does not consist necessarily or even primarily of legally relevant components. In any case, sociology does not recognize
a "behaving" (*acting*) collective personality. When sociology uses

the terms "state," "nation," "corporation," "family," "army division" or similarly collective concepts, it does so merely to focus on
a certain kind of development of alternative modes of social behavior by individual persons. Thus the legal terminology, which is
used because of its precision and usage, obtains here a completely
different meaning.

b.)   The interpretation of behavior also has to take into account a
most important vital fact: these collective concepts derived from
legal, common sense or any other technical ideas, are meaningful
to individuals either because they exist at least partially or because
they represent something with a normative authority. This is true
not only of judges and of bureaucrats but of the public at large as
well. Individuals orient their conduct to them and in this way they
very often exercise a very real, dominating causal influence on the
course of behavior of these individuals. Especially is this true
where these concepts are part of a recognized positive or negative
pattern. The modern *state* represents to a not inconsiderable degree a complex of concerted action on the part of individual persons as well, because many people act in the belief that it exists or
should exist in precisely this way to provide legal validity for the
issuance of its orders. This will be discussed further below.
Though it would be possible for sociological terminology to elimi-
nate these concepts from common usage as being too pedantic and
all-inclusive and substitute new terms, it would be, at least in the
present context quite out of the question.

c.)   There is finally the method of the so-called organic school of
sociology, of which Schaeffle's brilliant work, *Bau und Leben des
sozialen Koerpers*, represents a classical example. This school attempts to explain social interaction by using as its premise the
"whole" (e.g., economics) to which the individual's behavior is
related and then interpreted. This process is similar to the way in
which a physiologist would analyze the role of a bodily organ within the community of organisms, i.e., how it contributes toward the
survival of the rest of the organism. In this context there may be
recalled the famous dictum of a physiologist during a seminar:
"Paragraph X:" he said, "the Spleen. Gentlemen we know nothing
about the spleen. So much for the spleen." Of course, a great deal
was "known" about the spleen, such as position, size, shape, etc.;

only its "functions" could not be ascertained and this absence of knowledge he characterized as ignorance. To what extent other disciplines regard this manner of functional analysis of the parts of a whole as definitive need not be discussed here; but it is well-known that biochemical and biophysical forms of analysis of the organism are not exhausted with such a functional approach.

For purposes of sociological analysis such an approach is of importance because it serves first as a convenient point of departure for purposes of demonstration, as well as for provisional orientation. In this form it may be highly useful and even necessary— but at the same time, if its empirical value is overestimated, or if it is simply overconceptualized, the advantages of such an approach are lost. Secondly, it may be the only way under certain circumstances of determining just what processes of social behavior are necessary for our understanding in order to explain a particular phenomenon. It is at this stage that the real task of sociology, as we understand it, begins.

In the case of social collectivities we are especially in a position to create something that goes beyond the demonstration of the functional relationships and uniformities usually found in physical or biological organisms. Unlike the process in the natural sciences, we can here obtain a subjective interpretation of the behavior of the individuals directly involved. This is so because the natural sciences are limited to the formulation of causal uniformities in objects and events and to the explanation of individual facts by applying them. We do not really "understand" the behavior of cells but merely recognize their functional relationship, on the basis of which we then introduce a generalization. This additional success of explanation by interpretative understanding, rather than by mere empirical observation, is of course obtained at a price, which is the essentially hypothetical and fragmentary character of the results achieved in this manner. Still, it is precisely this kind of subjective understanding which provides sociological analysis with its distinct character.

This is not the place to discuss also the extent to which the behavior of animals becomes subjectively understandable to us or our behavior to them; such understanding is highly uncertain and its application most problematical. But insofar as such understanding exists, it would be conceivable to formulate a sociology of the relations of man to animals, both domestic and wild. It is true, after all, that many animals "understand" orders, wrath, love, aggressiveness and react to them not merely instinctively and mechanically but consciously meaningful and on the basis of previous experience. Our own ability to identify ourselves with the behavior of primitive peoples is hardly likely to be any better. But neither do we have any reliable means of determining the subjective state of mind of any animal or if we do, it is at best very unsatisfactory.

The problems of animal psychology are known for being interesting as well as difficult. It is also known that there are animal social organizations of many kinds: monogamous and polygamous "families;" herds, flocks, and even "states" with a functional division of labor. The extent of functional differentiation of these animal societies by no means parallels that of the organic or morphological differentiation of individual members of the species. For example, the functional differentiation found among termites, and therefore that of the products of their social organization, is far more advanced than that found among the ants and bees. Here it may well be that the observer must be satisfied with achieving a purely functional analysis. Such an analysis would enable him to study the means which the species regards as indispensable for its survival: nutrition, defense, reproduction and reconstruction, and to identify those animals charged with the execution of these and other functions, i.e., kings and queens, workers, soldiers, drones, propagators, substitute queens, etc. Anything beyond that would remain for a long time merely speculation or investigations of the extent to which heredity on the one hand and environment on the other, would be involved in the development of these "social" proclivities. This was particularly true of the controversies between Goette and Weisman. Weisman's concept of the omnipotence of natural selection was based largely on wholly non-empirical deductions. Still, all serious authorities are agreed that the reduction to a functional level of analysis is simply a necessity and will, it is hoped, be of a purely temporary character. (Compare, for example, on the state of knowledge of the termites, the study by Escherich, 1909). We would like to know not only the significance of the functions of these many differentiated types for survival, but also how, for example, the theory of the inheritance of acquired characteristics—or its opposite—bears on the problem of explaining the origins of these differentiations, as well as the influence of different variants on that theory. In addition, it would be well to know first what factors are decisive for the original differentiation of specialized types from the still neutral undifferentiated species type; second, what causes the individual once it is differentiated to act in a manner calculated to bring about the survival of the differentiated group. Wherever some progress has been made in the research on these problems, it occurred through experimental demonstration of the probability regarding the role of chemical stimuli or physiological processes such as nutritional habits, effects of parasitic castration, etc., in the case of individual organisms. How far there is even the ghost of a chance to make the existence of "psychological" (i.e., subjective) or meaningful orientation experimentally possible, even the expert would hardly venture to guess.

A verifiable presentation of the psyche of these social animals lending itself to meaningful understanding would appear to be attainable even as an ideal goal only within very narrow limits. At any rate, we cannot expect to obtain from this source any real contribution to the understanding of human social behavior. On the contrary—in the field of animal psychology human analogy will and ought to be used cautiously. We may expect, however, that some day such biological analogies will be useful in suggesting significant new approaches. For example, they may throw light on the question of how in the early stages of human social differentiation the impact of mechanical and instinctive factors must be calculated in, as compared to that of those factors which are accessible to subjective interpretation generally and, more specifically, to that of consciously rational behavior. Interpretative sociology will have to be made to recognize that for early human development it is the impact of the first set of factors which is of decisive importance and that even in the later stages recognition must be had of their continuous interaction with others.

Traditional behavior and especially charismatic behavior often carry the seeds of psychic contagion and thereby act as transmission belts for many evolutionary stimuli of the social process. Such types of behavior are closely related to phenomena that can be understood either solely in biological terms or are subject to incomplete interpretation in terms of subjective motives, fusing almost imperceptibly into the biological. None of this relieves sociology of the obligation to accomplish, even within such narrow limits, what only it alone can do.

The various works by Othman Spann are rich in suggestive ideas along these lines, though frequently he too errs on the side of pure value judgments that are not part of a true empirical investigation. Nevertheless, he is undoubtedly right in his emphasis on the importance of a functional point of view for the preliminary investigation of a social problem; this is what he calls "universalist method."

What we need to know primarily is what kind of behavior is functional in terms of survival and, above all, necessary for the continuation of cultural uniqueness and the continuity of the corresponding types of social behavior, before we can inquire into its origins and motivation. First, we need to know what a king, an official, an entrepreneur, a procurer, a magician, a producer does: i.e., what kind of behavior is typical and important enough to justify his being classified in any of these categories and is therefore relevant to analysis prior to the beginning of such analysis. (This is what H. Rickert means by value judgment.) But it is only such analysis which achieves understanding of the behavior of typically differentiated human (and only human) individuals and therefore is to be considered the specific function of sociology.

It is in any case a tremendous misunderstanding to assume that an individualistic methodology presupposes also an individualistic system of values. This assumption is as faulty as the related one of confusing the relatively unavoidable tendency of social concepts to acquire a rational character with the belief that rational motives always predominate or that rationalism can be positively evaluated.

Even a socialist economy would be individualistic for purposes of sociological analysis. That is, it must be understood on the basis of individual behavior—for example that of the functionaries who run it; and this would be equally true in the case of a free market system which is analyzed in terms of the theory of marginal utility, though it might be possible to find a more suitable but still similar method. Truly empirical sociological investigation begins only with the question, what did and still does motivate the individual functionaries and members of the community to conduct themselves in such a way as to bring about the creation of this "community" and to insure its continuation? Any formal functional analysis that uses the 'whole' as its point of departure can accomplish only preliminary preparations for further investigation; its utility and indispensability is, if it is properly applied, of course incontestable.

10.   The various sociological generalizations which it is customary to identify as "scientific laws," as for example, Gresham's Law, are in fact typical probabilities confirmed by observation. The assumption is that under certain given conditions a projected course of action will occur which will be intelligible in terms of typical motives and of the typical subjective intentions of those engaged in a certain behavior. These generalizations are both understandable and definitive to the highest degree insofar as the typically observed course of behavior can be understood in terms of the purely rational pursuit of a goal, or where for reasons of methodological convenience such a theoretical type can be heuristically employed; in such cases the relationship between means and ends is clearly understood empirically, especially where the choice of means was "inevitable." In such an instance it can be legitimately stated that insofar as the conduct was strictly goal-oriented it could not have taken any other direction. The reasons would be primarily technical, since, given the clearly defined ends, no other means were available to the individuals engaged in such behavior. Such a case shows emphatically how mistaken it is to regard any kind of psychology as the ultimate foundation of the sociological interpretation of human behavior. To be sure, everybody appears today to have his own interpretation of psychology. Certain definite methodological purposes justify a treatment of certain types of process which attempts to follow the procedures of the natural sciences, separating the "physical" from the "psychic" phenomena in a manner quite alien to the disciplines concerned with human behavior.

The results of psychological investigation which employs the methods of the natural sciences in any number of possible ways may, naturally, just like those of any other science, have, within certain limits, great significance for sociological problems; and indeed this has happened frequently. However, such use of psychological data must be distinguished from any investigation of human behavior in terms of its subjective meaning. Consequently, sociology does not bear any closer logical relationship to psychology than to any other science. The fault here lies with a concept of "psychic" which regards everything nonphysical as *ipso facto* psychic; yet the real meaning of the solution of a mathematical problem by a person is not a "psychic" process: the rational deliberations by an individual, whether or not the results of a certain contemplated course of conduct will promote certain specific interests, together with the corresponding decision, do not become one iota more intelligible on the basis of psychological considerations. Yet it is precisely such rational assumptions on which rest most of the laws of sociology as well as of economics. On the other hand, in explaining irrational conduct sociologically, interpretive psychology (i.e., the form which uses subjective understanding) undoubtedly can be of decisive value. But this does not change the fundamental methodological situation.

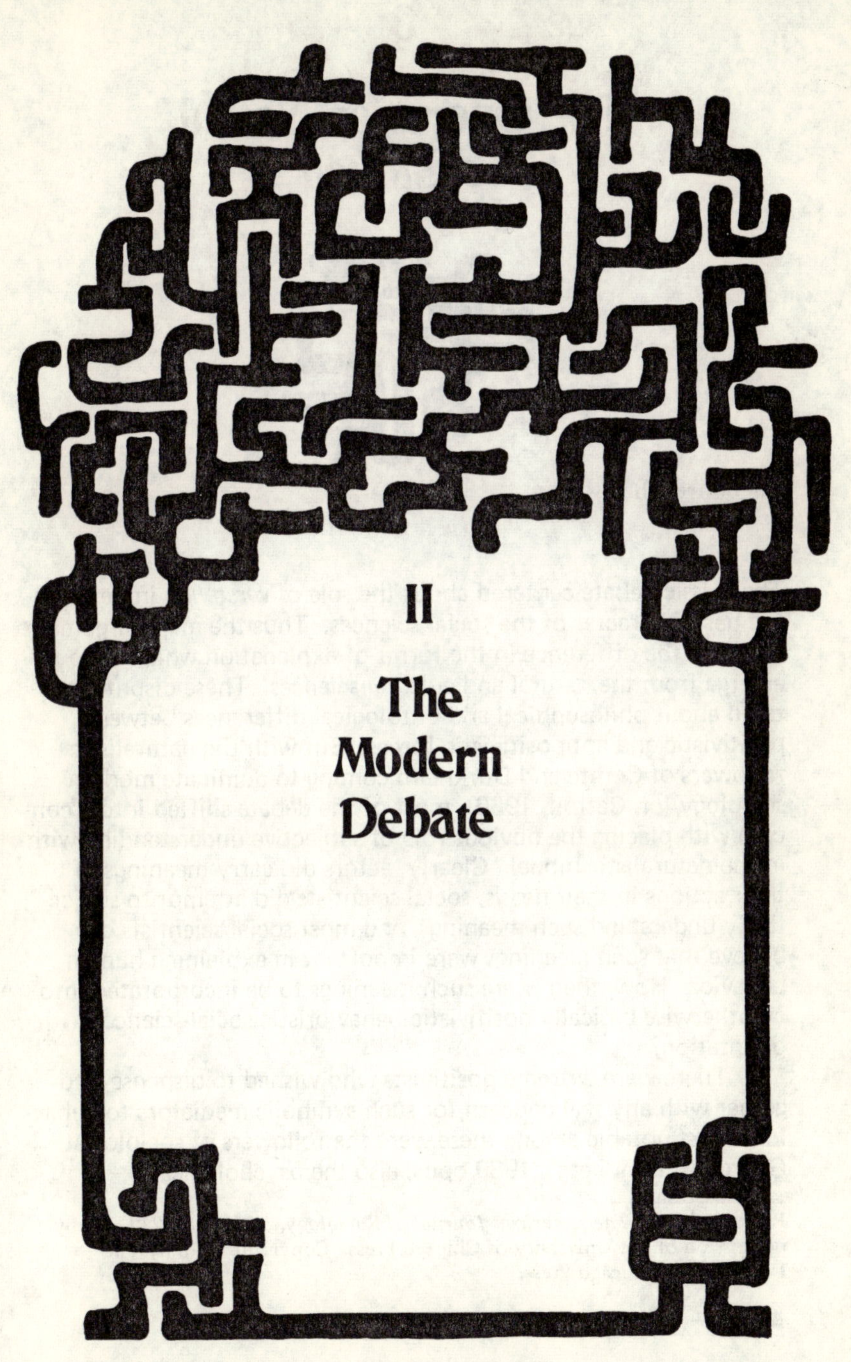
II
The
Modern
Debate

3

The Operation Called
Verstehen

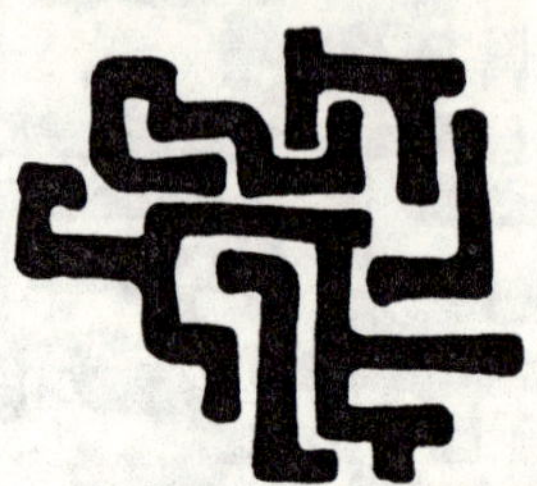

Theodore Abel

The classic debate centered about the role of *verstehen* in defining
the basic character of the social sciences. Thus the major argument
was over the difference in the forms of explanation which were to
emerge from the natural and cultural sciences. These disputes centered about philosophical and ontological differences between
positivistic and antipositivistic forces. But with the naturalistic
followers of Comte and Durkheim coming to dominate modern
sociology (cf. Catton, 1966), most of the debate shifted into a concern with placing the obvious role of subjective understanding within the naturalistic model. Clearly, actors did carry meanings of
their actions in their heads, social scientists did attempt to subjectively understand such meanings, and most social scientists did
believe that such meanings were important in explaining human
behavior. How, then, were such meanings to be incorporated into
an otherwise basically positivistic-behavioristic social-science
orientation?

There were extreme positivists who wished to dispense altogether with any real concern for such symbolic mediators to behavior. Most notable among these were the followers of sociologist
George A. Lundberg's 1939 opus; also the psychological

Reprinted from *The American Journal of Sociology, 54* (1948), 211–18, by
permission of the University of Chicago Press. Copyright 1948 by The
University of Chicago Press.

disciples of behavioristic psychologist John B. Watson, especially today's followers of B. F. Skinner.) However, most social scientists continued to concern themselves with the role of meanings in social life.

The *verstehen* tradition was carried forward by the followers of Charles Horton Cooley (1864–1929) and George Herbert Mead (1863–1931). Although Cooley followed an extreme introspective emphasis,[1] Mead tried to bridge a concern with symbolic mediation in man's actions with a naturalistic pragmatism that prompted him to call his position Social Behaviorism.[2] Mead's work, along with the more purely sociological emphases of William Isaac Thomas (1863–1947),[3] was to form the cornerstone of a major orientation in contemporary sociology usually called *Symbolic Interactionism.*[4] A similar movement from an initially more introspective concern with subjective understanding "validated as causal by our own experience" to a more naturalistic-positivistic perspective in the macrosociological sphere could be observed in the work of Robert M. MacIver (1882–).[5] Another noteworthy case of contemporary emphasis on *verstehen* which deserves mention was the delineation of the *logico-meaningful* method expounded by Pitirim A. Sorokin (1889–1968).[6] Although Sorokin began his writing with a behavioristic emphasis, he shifted his concern towards a more mentalistic emphasis in his later writings.[7] Nonetheless, Sorokin did not – as many of his critics have accused him – consider subjective understanding to be self-validating; it had to be validated through the normal causal evaluation process. Thus Sorokin, too, represents an attempt to bridge the earlier Idealism with the growing movement towards positivistic naturalism.

In the following essay, one which has had widespread circulation and reaction, Theodore Abel (1896–) attempted an interpretation of the *verstehen* concept in conformity with positivistic criteria for validation.[8] This paper has gained widespread acceptance within modern sociology and probably represents the dominant interpretation found today, at least within American sociology.

—MT

NOTES

1. Good brief overviews of Cooley's contributions and method can be found in Coser (1971), pp. 305–30 and Angell (1968). Cooley's method of "sympathetic understanding" is outlined in Cooley (1930).

2.   The major works relavant to sociology are: Mead (1934, 1938) and Reck (1964). For an evaluation of Mead, see Natanson (1956) and Meltzer (1959).

3.   Regarding Thomas' life and work, see Young (n.d.) and Janowitz (1966). For a more modern use of Thomas' famous dictum ("If men define situations as real, they are real in their consequences.") see Stebbins (1969).

4.   Regarding this tradition and its variations, see Kuhn (1964) and Blumer (1969).

5. See MacIver (1942). Regarding MacIver's shift towards naturalism over the years, see Catton (1966) pp. 96–113.

6.   Cf. Sorokin (1937-a). For criticism, see Bierstedt (1937) with Sorokin's "Rejoinder..." (1937-b) and Silvers (1966).

7.   Regarding Sorokin's earlier positivism, see Isajiw (1956). The clearest statement by Sorokin on the need to empirically verify *logical-meaningful* integration through causal analysis is unfortunately in an out-of-the-way source which has received scant attention, Sorokin (1946).

8.   For his latest statement on the *verstehen* problem, see Abel (1970) pp. 67–71.

The advocates of *Verstehen* define it as a singular form of operation which we perform whenever we attempt to explain human behavior. The idea behind this claim is by no means of German origin. Long before Dilthey and Weber, Vico acclaimed mathematics and human history as subjects about which we have a special kind of knowledge. This he attributed to the fact that the abstractions and fictions of mathematics are created by us, while history, too, is "made by men." He claimed that human beings can possess a type of knowledge concerning things they themselves produce which is not obtainable about the phenomena of nature.

Comte, too, implied that a special procedure is involved in the interpretation of human behavior. He held that the methods used in sociology embrace not only observation and experiment but a further process of verification which makes use of what he vaguely referred to as "our knowledge of human nature." According to him, empirical generalizations about human behavior are not valid unless they are in accord with our knowledge of human nature. Comte was the first to establish what may be termed "the postulate of *Verstehen*" for sociological research, for he asserted that no sociological demonstration is complete until the conclusions of historical and statistical analyses are in harmony with the "laws of human nature."

In the American sociological field Cooley is the outstanding protagonist of the idea that we understand the human and the social in ways different from those in which we understand the material. His theory is that we can understand the behavior of human beings by being able to share their "state of mind." This ability to share other people's minds is a special knowledge, distinct from the kind of perception gleaned from tests and statistics. Statistical knowledge without "emphatic" knowledge is superficial and unintelligent. Between the two, Cooley claims, "there is a difference in kind which it would be fatuous to overlook."[2]

The notion of *Verstehen* is included in Znaniecki's concept of the "humanistic coefficient" and particularly in the role he ascribes to "vicarious experience" as a source of sociological data. According to Znaniecki, vicarious experience enables the student of human behavior "to gain a specific kind of information which the natural experimenter . . . ignores altogether."[3]

Similarly, Sorokin stresses the need for *Verstehen* when he insists that the causal-functional method is not applicable to the interpretation of cultural phenomena. He points out that the social sciences must employ the logico-meaningful method which enables us to perceive connections which "are much more intimately comprehensible, more readily perceived, than are causal-functional unities."[4]

MacIver, too, speaks of a special method which must be used whenever we study social causation. He calls this process "imaginative reconstruction." He claims the causal formula of classical mechanics cannot be applied to human behavior. However, the student of human behavior will find this compensated for by "the advantage that some of the factors operative in social causation are understandable as causes; are validated as causal by our own experience."[5]

As these brief references indicate, there is no dearth of tradition and authority behind the idea of *Verstehen*.[6] It is, therefore, surprising to find that, while many social scientists have eloquently discoursed on the existence of a special method in the study of human behavior, none has taken the trouble to describe the nature of this method. They have given it various names; they have insisted on its use; they have pointed to it as a special kind of operation which has no counterpart in the physical sciences; and they have extolled its superiority as a process of giving insight unobtainable by any other methods. Yet the advocates of *Verstehen* have continually neglected to specify how this operation of "understanding" is performed—and what is singular about it. What, exactly, do we do when we say we practice *Verstehen?* What significance can we give to results achieved by *Verstehen?* Unless the operation is clearly defined, *Verstehen* is but a vague notion, and, without being dogmatic, we are unable to ascertain how much validity can be attributed to the results achieved by it.

I. THE OPERATION ILLUSTRATED

Our first task is to ascertain the formula according to which the operation of *Verstehen* is performed. To do so, we had best examine a few illustrations of behavior analysis. For this purpose we shall use three examples: the first will deal with a single case; the second, with a generalization; and the third, with a statistical regularity.

Case I. Last April 15 a freezing spell suddenly set in, causing a temperature drop from 60 to 34 degrees. I saw my neighbor rise from his desk by the window, walk to the woodshed, pick up an ax, and chop some wood. I then observed him carrying the wood into the house and placing it in the fireplace. After he had lighted the wood, he sat down at his desk and resumed his daily task of writing.

From these observations I concluded that, while working, my neighbor began to feel chilly and, in order to get warm, lighted a fire. This conclusion has all the earmarks of an "obvious fact." Yet it is obvious only because I have fitted the action of my neighbor into a sequential pattern by assuming that the stimulus "drop in temperature" induced the response "making a fire." Since I recognize a relevant connection between the response and the stimulus, I state that I understand the behavior of my neighbor. I may even say that I am certain of it ("The case is obvious"), provided I note carefully to what this certainty refers. I *cannot* be certain that this is the *correct* or true explanation of his conduct. To be sure my explanation is correct, I need additional information. I can go over to him and ask him why he lighted the fire. He may confirm my interpretation. However, I cannot stop there. Suppose he has another, hidden, intention? He may be expecting a guest and wish to show off his fireplace. Or suppose he himself is not aware of the "true" motive? Perhaps he was impelled by a subconscious motive of wanting to burn down his house so as to punish the fellow who harasses him about paying off the mortgage. If so, his lighting the fire would have a symbolic function. Of what, then, am I certain? I am certain only that my interpretation *could* be correct.

Hence, *Verstehen* gives me the certainty that a given interpretation of behavior is a possible one. I *know* that it can happen this way, even though I cannot be certain that such was the case in this instance. My interpretation in itself is not a hypothesis; only its application to the stated case is hypothetical.

Whence comes this certainty that I achieve through *Verstehen?* Since the case is simple, the answer is simple: I have enacted it myself. Feeling chilled, I have gathered wood and lighted a fire; therefore, I *know*. The sense of relevance is the result of personal experience; the connection has been established by me before, so I am *certain* of its possibility.

However, the answer as stated does not give us a clear picture of the operation the act of *Verstehen* involves. It will, therefore, be necessary to schematize the evidence and show the steps taken to perform the operation.

Two sets of observations are given in our example. First, there is a sequence of bodily movement (chopping wood, lighting a fire, etc.); second, there is a thermometer reading of a near-freezing temperature. The act of *Verstehen* links these two facts into the conclusion that the freezing weather was the stimulus which set off the response "making a fire." An elementary examination shows that three items of information are utilized to reach this conclusion:

1. Low temperature (A) reduces the temperature of the body (B).
2. Heat is produced (C) by making a fire (D).
3. A person "feeling cold" (B') will "seek warmth" (C').

Through this interpretation the three items are linked together as follows:

$$A-B \qquad\qquad\qquad C-D$$
$$B'-C'$$

We immediately recognize the third item as the significant element of the interpretation. The two conditions $(A-B)$, together with their known consequences $(C-D)$, are disparate facts. We link them into a sequence and state that $C-D$ is the consequence of $A-B$ by "translating" B and C into feeling-states of a human organism, namely, B' and C'. Introducing these intervening factors enables us to apply a generalization concerning the function of the organism (behavior maxim), from which we deduce the drop in temperature as a possible "cause" of my neighbor's behavior.

By specifying the steps which are implicit in the interpretation of our case, we have brought out two particulars which are characteristic of the act of *Verstehen*. One is the "internalizing" of observed factors in a given situation; the other is the application of a behavior maxim which makes the connection between these factors relevant. Thus we "understand" a given human action if we can apply to it a generalization based upon personal experience. We can apply such a rule of behavior if we are able to "internalize" the facts of the situation.

These propositions require further elucidation, but, before we attempt this, let us consider two other examples of behavior analysis.

Case 2. In one of Lundberg's articles we find the following generalization:

> Faced by the insecurity of a changing and hostile world, we seek security by creating "eternal verities" in our thoughts. The more inadequate we feel, the more we indulge in this type of wishful thinking. Conversely, as the clergy has always complained, in times of prosperity and security, man tends to neglect his gods. It has been suggested that the Platonic preference for the changeless may be due to the fact that the Greeks did not have a mathematical technique such as the calculus for dealing with modes and rates of change.[7]

The opening sentence of this quotation asserts a relevant connection between "belief in eternal verities" (verbal response) and "a changing and hostile world" (stimulus). The subsequent sentences hint at a possible statistical basis for the generalization and cite two historical examples as illustrations. Clearly there is insufficient evidence to substantiate the validity of the interpretation as a tendency in some of us toward idealistic philosophy. We can recognize, though, that the connection asserted by the generalization is relevant; that is, we "understand" it, and so consider it possible.

The act of *Verstehen* which is implied here involves the same operation we have observed in the first example. We internalize "change and hostility" (B), which we observe to be an attribute of "the world" (A), into "feeling of inadequacy" (B'). The connotation "changeless" (C), which the concept "eternal verities" (D) implies, we internalize into "feeling of security" (C'). Having thus internalized the situation, we can now apply the behavior maxim that a person who feels inadequate (when facing change) will seek security (in something changeless). This procedure provides the mediating links $B'-C'$, which enable us to "understand," or recognize, the relevancy of the causal connection brought out in the generalization.

Case 3. Competent statistical research has established a high correlation $(r=.93)$ between the annual rate of crop production and the rate of marriage in a given year. There are, of course, statistical methods for proving whether or not this correlation is spurious. In this case, however, we feel that we can forego such tests because the correlation as such does not present a problem to us. We regard the connection as relevant; in short, we say we "understand" why the rate of marriage in farming districts closely follows the rate of crop production.

The act of *Verstehen* which this reasoning implies can be shown to involve the same procedure we have observed in the other examples. We use as items of information the fact that failure of crops (A) materially lowers the farmer's income (B) and the fact that one is making new commitments (C) when one marries (D). We then internalize B into "feeling of anxiety" (B') and C—since the behavior in question is "postponement of marriage"—into "fear of new commitments" (C'). We are now able to apply the behavior maxim: "People who experience anxiety will fear new commitments" $(B'-C')$. Since we can fit the fact of fewer marriages when crops fail into this rule, we say we "understand" the correlation.

II. THE OPERATION ANALYZED

The examples show that the characteristic feature of the operation of *Verstehen* is the postulation of an intervening process "located" inside the human organism, by means of which we recognize an observed—or assumed—connection as relevant or "meaningful." *Verstehen*, then, consists of the act of bringing to the foreground the inner-organic sequence intervening between a stimulus and a response.

The examples also suggest that there are special conditions which determine the need for making the intervening process explicit. Some connections appear to be obvious; that is, we recognize their relevancy instantaneously and without any awareness of the implicit assumptions upon which the recognition is based. These are usually connections of which we have direct knowledge, because we ourselves established such connections in the past; or they are connections we have previously examined, so that their occurrence is accepted as an expected or familiar happening.

The need for making the intervening process explicit arises whenever behavior is not routine or commonplace. This is clearly the case when we are puzzled. For example, when we were confronted with the evidence that in army units in which promotion was easy there was much more griping about "injustice" than in those units in which very few were promoted, we were puzzled. We would expect the contrary. It is only by internalizing the situation—namely, by introducing the intervening factor of "expectation"—that we are able to understand the connection. If we then assume that in units in which promotion is easy there will be greater expectation of promotion, we can apply the behavior maxim: "The higher one's expectations, the greater one's disappointment if those expectations are not fulfilled." This enables us to "understand" the seemingly paradoxical behavior.

Another condition for making the intervening inner-organic sequence explicit arises whenever we are called upon to explain the reason for asserting a connection between occurrences. This is particularly so when no experimental or statistical data are available and recourse is taken to arguments in support of an interpretation. This happens frequently when interpretations of individual historical events are attempted, as, for example, establishing the cause of a war. Here the behavior in question can be related to earlier events

solely on the basis that in terms of assumed feeling-states such a relation is a plausible one.

As has been indicated, the operation of *Verstehen* involves
three steps: (1) internalizing the stimulus, (2) internalizing the
response, and (3) applying behavior maxims. The questions now
arise as to how to go about the process in internalizing and where
we get our knowledge of behavior maxims.

1. Internalizing the Stimulus

To the best of my knowledge, no one has yet specified a technique
by which we can objectively attribute certain feeling-states to persons faced by a particular situation of event. The arbitrary procedure we employ to internalize a stimulus consists of *imagining*
what emotions may have been aroused by the impact of a given
situation or event. Sometimes we are able to employ definite clues
which we have gathered while observing the impact. These may
have been gestures, facial expressions, or exclamations or comments.
Where there are no such clues, we note the effect produced by an
event or situation. Then we imagine how we would have been affected by such an impact. For example, not being a farmer, I never
experienced the consequence of crop failure. However, observing
that its effect is a curtailment of income, I attribute to the farmer a
feeling of anxiety which I recall having felt—or imagine I might feel—
under similar circumstances. Thus the internalizing of a stimulus
depends largely upon our ability to describe a situation or event by
categorizing it and evoking a personal experience which fits into
that category.

2. Internalizing the Response

Here, too, no specific techniques are known which permit a definite
association between feeling-states and observed behavior. All that
can again be said is that we use our imagination when we ascribe a
motive to a person's behavior—for example, "fear of new commitments" as the reason for postponing marriage; or, in another instance, when we view the behavior as expressive of some emotion
—namely, when we infer that the "griping" of soldiers over promo-
tions evokes a feeling of disappointment. We generally infer the
motive of an act from the known or observed modification it
produces. If we express this consequence of an act in general terms,

we can utilize our personal experience with motives or feelings we had when we ourselves acted in order to produce a similar result.

In cases where both stimulus and response are stated, imagination is facilitated by the fact that both can be viewed as part of a complete situation. This enables us to relate to each other whatever inferences we make about the stimulus and the response. We then select the inferences which "fit" one another in such a way that the given behavior can be recognized as the "solution" (release of tension) of the "problem" (tension experience) created by the impact of the stated event.

3. Behavior Maxims

The generalizations which we call "behavior maxims" link two feeling-states together in a uniform sequence and imply a functional dependence between them. In the cases cited it can be seen that the functional dependence consists of the fact that the feeling-state we ascribe to a given human action is *directed* by the feeling-state we presume is evoked by an impinging situation or event. Anxiety directs caution; a feeling of cold, the seeking of warmth; a feeling of insecurity, a desire for something that will provide reassurance.

Behavior maxims are not recorded in any textbooks on human behavior. In fact, they can be constructed *ad hoc* and be acceptable to us as propositions even though they have not been established experimentally. The relation asserted appears to us as self-evident.

This peculiarity of behavior maxims can be accounted for only by the assumption that they are ganeralizations of direct personal experience derived from introspection and self-observation. Such personal experiences appear originally in the form of what Alexander has called "emotional syllogisms." He has this to say about them:

> Our understanding of psychological connections is based on the tacit recognition of certain causal relationships which we know from everyday experience and the validity of which we accept as self-evident. We understand anger and aggressive behavior as a reaction to an attack; fear and guilt as results of aggressiveness; envy as an outgrowth of the feeling of weakness and inadequacy. Such self-evident connections as "I hate him because he attacks me" I shall call emotional syllo-

gisms. The feeling of the self-evident validity of these emotional connections is derived from daily introspective experience as we witness the emotional sequences in ourselves.... Just as the logic of intellectual thinking is based on repeated and accumulated experiences of relations in the external world, the logic of emotions is based on the accumulated experiences of our own emotional reactions. [8]

Emotional syllogisms when stated in the form of general propositions are behavior maxims. This explains their familiar ring and accounts for the facility with which they can be formulated. In generalizing emotional syllogisms we proceed on the assumption that the emotions of others function similarly to our own.

We find, then, that in all its essential features the operation of *Verstehen* is based upon the application of personal experience to observed behavior. We "understand" an observed or assumed connection if we are able to parallel either one with something we know though self-observation does happen. Furthermore, since the operation consists of the application of knowledge we already possess, it cannot serve as a means of discovery. At best it can only confirm what we already know.

III. THE OPERATION EVALUATED

From the foregoing description of the operation of *Verstehen* we can draw several inferences as to its limitations and possibilities. The most obvious limitation of the operation is its dependence upon knowledge derived from personal experience. The ability to define behavior will vary with the amount and quality of the personal experience and the introspective capacity of the interpreter. It will also depend upon his ability to generalize his experiences. In some cases it may be possible to secure objective data on the basis of which the verification of an interpretation can be approximated. However, owing to the relative inaccessibility of emotional experiences, most interpretations will remain mere expressions of opinion, subject only to the "test" of plausibility.

Regardless of the relative ability of people to use it, a second limitation to the use of the operation itself lies in the fact that it is *not a method of verification*. This means that what in the realm of scientific research we consider a quality of crucial importance is not an attribute of the operation of *Verstehen*.

When we say we "understand" a connection, we imply nothing more than recognizing it as a possible one. We simply affirm that we have at least once in direct experience observed and established the connection or its equivalent. But from the affirmation of a possible connection we cannot conclude that it is also probable. From the point of view of *Verstehen* alone, any connection that is possible is *equally* certain. In any given case the test of the actual probability calls for the application of objective methods of observation; e.g., experiments, comparative studies, statistical operations of mass data, etc. We do not accept the fact that farmers postpone intended marriages when faced with crop failure because we can "understand" the connection. It is acceptable to us because we have found through reliable statistical operations that the correlation between the rate of marriage and the rate of crop production is extremely high. We would continue to accept the fact even if we could not "understand" it. In this instance the operation of *Verstehen* does no more than relieve us of a sense of apprehension which would undoubtedly haunt us if we were unable to understand the connection.

The postulate of *Verstehen* can now be viewed from a proper perspective. It cannot be made to imply that if we do not "understand" a connection it surely, or most probably, is false. It does, however, imply that our curiosity concerning human behavior does not rest until we have in some way been able to relate it to our personal experience. The satisfaction of curiosity produces subjective increment but adds nothing to the objective validity of a proposition. Thus, all assertions based solely on the evidence of "understandability" can be viewed as cases of "misplaced familiarity."

These limitations virtually preclude the use of the operation of *Verstehen* as a scientific tool of analysis. Still there is one positive function which the operation can perform in scientific investigations: It can serve as an aid in preliminary explorations of a subject. Furthermore, the operation can be particularly helpful in setting up hypotheses, even though it cannot be used to test them.

In dealing with human behavior, we create hypotheses whenever we ask for the "stimulus" which produced a given response, or when we attempt to predict what "response" will follow from a given occurrence. It is an accepted fact that, in formulating hypotheses, we start with some "hunch" or "intuition." Now it appears highly probable that the hunches which lead us to certain hypotheses concerning human behavior originate from the application of the operation of *Verstehen*. This follows from the fact that the operation—in addition to using the stated stimulus or response—allows the use of another item of knowledge (a behavior maxim), which permits us to "reach out" from a given observation to its unknown counterpart. The diagram representing the reasoning about the neighbor seen chopping wood clearly indicates how behavior maxims can serve as a source of "hunches." Suppose $C-D$ were given as an item of observation. By internalizing C, we obtain C', to which we can then apply a behavior maxim, which gives us B'. B', in turn, provides a clue to the nature of the situation or event which may be the possible stimulus ($A-B$) to the behavior question. Lundberg's generalization (Case 2) is an example of a hypothesis derived in this fashion. By postulating that people who assert "eternal verities" are seeking security, he inferred a strong feeling of anxiety as the counterpart to this motive. He then surmised that the "changing and hostile world" might be the anxiety-producing condition. A "hunch" similarly reached was used by Durkheim in his study of suicide. When he found the rate of suicide varying in different groups, he was confronted by the problem of selecting the most likely determinant from a multitude of attributes of group life. From Merton's statement of the "paradigm of Durkheim's theoretic analysis," we can infer that Durkheim first internalized rates of suicide as "functions of unrelieved anxieties and stresses to which persons are subjected."[9] He then viewed such emotional states as the result of a lack of "psychic support," such as is provided by intimate associations with others. This suggested the possibility of social cohesion being the crucial factor which determines the characteristic rate of suicide in a group. Subsequent investigations established a high degree of probability for this inference because Durkheim was able to show that the rate of suicide varies consistently in inverse ratio with the degree of group coherence.

By reversing the procedure, we arrive at hunches about possible responses to given or expected occurrences. That is, we internalize the situation by projecting it as a problem experience and then, by means of a behavior maxim, infer the problem-solving response (intention). However, to guess the particular form the response will take requires information which the operation of *Verstehen* does not provide. It would not, for example, be of use in trying to conjecture specific ways and means of aggression which may be employed by a group in response to a provocation by another group. The operation gives us "hunches," and it points out the general character of possible factors, but it does not enable us to evaluate probabilities.

The findings with regard to the operation of *Verstehen* may be summarized in the following propositions:

The operation of *Verstehen* is performed by analyzing a behavior situation in such a way—usually in terms of general "feeling-states"—that it parallels some personal experience of the interpreter.

Primarily the operation of *Verstehen* does two things: It relieves us of a sense of apprehension in connection with behavior that is unfamiliar or unexpected and it is a sourse of "hunches," which help us in the formulation of hypotheses.

The operation of *Verstehen* does not, however, add to our store of knowledge, because it consists of the application of knowledge already validated by personal experience; nor does it serve as a means of verification. The probability of a connection can be ascertained only by means of objective, experimental, and statistical tests.

NOTES

1. To avoid confusion, we prefer to use the German term instead of its English equivalent, which is "understanding." Understanding is a general term approximating the German *Begreifen* and does not convey the specific meaning intended by the term *Verstehen*, which implies a particular kind of understanding, applicable primarily to human behavior. Understanding is synonymous with comprehension, and Lundberg is perfectly right when he asserts (in *Foundations of Sociology* [New York: Macmillan Co., 1939], p. 51) that "understanding is the end at which all methods aim, rather than a method in itself." In this sense "understanding" is the goal of all sciences. *Verstehen*, on the other hand, is viewed by its proponents as a

method by means of which we can explain human behavior. The purpose of this paper is to clarify this point and evaluate its significance.

2. H. E. Cooley, *Sociological Theory and Social Research* (New York: Scribner's, 1930), p. 290.

3. Florian Znaniecki, *The Method of Sociology* (New York: Farrar & Rinehart, 1934), p. 167.

4. Pitirim Sorokin, *Social and Cultural Dynamics* (New York: American Book Co., 1937), p. 26.

5. R. M. MacIver, *Social Causation* (Boston: Ginn & Co., 1942) p. 263.

6. The more important works dealing with *Verstehen* are K. Bühler, *Die Krise der Philosophie* (Jena: Fischer, 1927); W. Dilthey, *Ideen ueber eine beschreibende und zergliedernde Psychologie* (Leipzig: Teubner, 1894); T. Erisman, *Die Eigenart des Geistigen* (Leipzig: Quelle, 1924); P. Häberlin, *Der Geist und die Triebe* (Berlin: Springer, 1924); K. Jaspers, *Allgemeine Psychopathologie* (Berlin: Springer, 1920); H. Rickert, *Die Grenzen der naturwissenschaftlichen Begriffsbildung* (Tübingen: Mohr, 1913); E. Rothacker, *Logik und Systematik der Geisteswissenschaften* (Bonn: Bouvier, 1947); G. Simmel, *Geschichtsphilosophie* (Berlin: Duncan, 1920); E. Spranger, *Lebensformen* (Halle: Niemeyer, 1924); and Max Weber, *Gesammelte Aufsaetze zur Wissenschaftslehre* (Tübingen: Mohr, 1920).

7. "Thoughtways of Contemporary Sociology," *American Sociological Review*, I (1936), 703.

8. Franz Alexander, "The Logic of Emotions and Its Dynamic Background," *International Journal of Psychoanalysis*, XVI (October 1935), 399.

9. R. K. Merton, "Sociological Theory," *American Journal of Sociology*, L (May 1945), 470.

4

Empirical Science and Max Weber's *Verstehende Soziologie*

Peter A. Munch

In recent years, philosophers have tended to differentiate between the contexts of *discovery* and *validation* (e.g., Rudner, 1966, pp.5–7). The former refers to the process of obtaining insights and hypotheses about the order of things. The latter refers to the methodological processes whereby such hypotheses are tested, evaluated, and verified. In general there seems to be no such thing as a *logic* of discovery; there are no rules one can best follow to come up with useful insights and hypotheses. The source of such ideas (whether from a dream or a programmed computer) is not an important issue in science. But the testing of such ideas empirically, many would argue, follows essentially the same rules (the same logic of validation) in all the sciences, social and natural alike.

In the preceding article, Abel argued that *verstehen* is a useful tool in the context of discovery. It gives insights and has heuristic value for the social sciences. But, according to Abel, it has no place in the context of validation.

In the following piece, Peter A. Munch argues a somewhat different case for the uses of *verstehen*. Munch believes that Abel has misunderstood Weber's goals in using *verstehen*. In its proper

From *American Sociological Review*, 22 (1957), 26–32. Reprinted by permission of the American Sociological Association and the author.

meaning asserts Munch, *verstehen* can be placed back into the context of validation.*

—MT

From time to time, Max Weber's *verstehende Soziologie* is scrutinized by sociologists. Recently Pierce[1] attempted to demonstrate the non-empirical nature of Weber's method of *Verstehen* but, in the writer's opinion, missed the mark, partly because of a peculiar conception of "empirical," partly because of an erroneous conception of Weber's method.

Pierce takes his starting point in "the necessity of distinguishing an experimentally testable assertion from a proposal to represent the observable facts by certain words or diagrams" (Conant as quoted by Pierce).[2] Taken out of context, Conant's statement seems clear enough. It is both valid and important to distinguish the *objective identification* of a factual object, property, condition, or event from its *symbolic representation:* The former is a procedure testable by experiment (controlled observation), the latter is a semantic procedure. In its original context, however, it is confusing to find the statement to be a comment to Robert Boyle's assertion that his *experimental demonstration* of what he named the "spring" of gases did not offer a *causal explanation* of the phenomenon.[3] This, too, is an important distinction but hardly expressable in terms of experimental testability as the discriminating criterion.

The "fundamental deficiency" of the Weberian position, according to Pierce, "stems . . . from the failure to distinguish verification of an empirical proposition from objective confirmation of a definition."[4] In the main, he appears to be thinking of the same sort of distinction that Conant had in mind, expressed in another connection as a distinction between a *definition* and an *empirical proposition.* [5] But, like Conant, he confuses the point by failing to distinguish a definition of a concept from its *application to an observable fact* and thereby ends up with a concept of "empirical" which is too narrow to be meaningful. Says Pierce:

---

*Munch's article is primarily a response to the previous article by Pierce in the same journal (1956). For Pierce's vigorous response to the Munch interpretation of his paper (an interpretation Pierce thought was quite inaccurate) see Pierce (1957).

It is important to understand that empirical veracity does not refer to the descriptive adequacy of the concepts which *identify* objects, events, conditions, or processes; neither does it refer to the conformity of properties of objects, events, conditions, or processes to a general statement in terms of which a given class of objects is merely identified. These conformities are matters of objective confirmation of definitions. Empirical veracity is a term which properly applies only to the adequacy with which propositions describe determinate *relationships* among *type* objects, events, conditions, or processes—which . . . already have been defined in terms that are *logically* independent both of each other and of the relationship predicated in the proposition.[6]

Thus, according to Pierce, the statement "This is a stone," is an "objective confirmation of a definition" but not an empirical proposition, "even if it be true,"[7] while the statement, "Birth rates vary inversely as real income," is an empirical proposition (even if it be false) "because the stated *relationship* can be verified or fail of verification, . . . independently of any *logical* connection between 'birth rates' and 'real income'."[8]

Pierce is here suggesting a conception of "empirical" which deviates strongly from the conventional meaning of the term. This is confusing, particularly since the proposed meaning purports to discriminate between types of procedure in scientific research which are not clearly distinguishable, while, on the other hand, it fails to distinguish where a distinction seems important.

"Empirical," according to its etymology and by general consensus (confirmed by all dictionaries), means "relating to or based on experience or observation" (Funk and Wagnalls). The only process in scientific research which is *purely* empirical, therefore, is the immediate apprehension of sense impressions. The *interpretation* of these sense impressions—which is necessary in order to translate them into a *perception* of factual objects, conditions, or events—is a mental process by which certain elements regarded as "characteristic" or "essential" are selected or abstracted from the immediately apprehended sense impressions while others are supplemented by inference and implication. A step further removed from the purely empirical observation of data is the thought process of *conception* whereby the properties or attributes of several perceived objects or events are analyzed, by means of further abstractions, and combined into more or less specific categories or types, which again may be fused, on the principle of identity or "sameness," into more general and increasingly abstract concepts. This may be referred to as the *analytical* aspect of the scientific procedure, the purpose of which is to determine the *properties* of observed phenomena and to classify them accordingly.

Still further removed from immediate sensation is the construction of "laws" and "principles" of a more or less general or inclusive nature, usually combining several objects, conditions, or events recurrently observed together. This is the essence of all scientific endeavor, and the end-goal is a complete rational comprehension of the total universe in terms of a cohesive theoretical system. But the laws and principles are in themselves nothing but rational—mathematical or logical—conjectures of "functional relationships" between certain categories of phenomena observed with some regularity to occur simultaneously or subsequently in space and time. We may refer to this aspect of the scientific procedure as its *hypothetical* aspect, the purpose of which is to establish a rationally consistent order in the universe in terms of functional or causal *relationships* between conceived categories of phenomena.

It is important to note, however, that the distinction between the analytical and the hypothetical aspects of scientific procedure cannot be drawn with a high degree of sharpness because "property" and "relationship" are not mutually exclusive concepts. Depending upon the level of analysis, the "properties" of any phenomenon may, from a different point of view, be regarded as "relationships" either between the specific parts of the phenomenon itself or between the phenomenon and more or less hypothetical external forces.

It follows from the preceding that a *purely* empirical science is a *contradictio in adjecto*. However, we generally refer to any thought process as "empirical" in so far as it is "relating to or based on" empirical observation, no matter how many steps removed from it. Only in this sense can we talk about *empirical sciences*: they are thereby distinguished from the *normative sciences*, whether rationally normative (such as all branches of pure mathematics, logic, and scientific methodology), morally normative (such as ethics and jurisprudence), or aesthetically normative (such as aesthetics in all its forms).

As rationality is the criterion of science in the sense that logic and mathematics are its tools, the scientific validity of a concept or proposition lies primarily in its logical consistency with a theoretical system which, in turn, is always based on some *a priori* principle of metaphysical nature. Only in the empirical sciences do we insist on the additional requirement that a concept or a proposition, as well as the theoretical system of which it is a part, should be consistent with human perception of "facts"—the basic metaphysical assumption being that human perception is a true reflection of a reality that can not only be subjected to a logically coherent system of interrelated concepts but, by its very nature, *is* such a system, only to be "discovered" by man.

What distinguishes the empirical sciences from other branches of human knowledge, then, is that their concepts and propositions (apart from their *a priori* principles) are ultimately referable to human perception.

"Empirical," as used by Pierce, fails to make this important distinction. Instead, it purports to discriminate between the analytical and the hypothetical aspects of scientific procedure, which, as we have seen, are not clearly distinguishable. The proposal apparently is to exclude from the term "empirical" the whole analytical aspect of the scientific procedure, both the theoretical definition of concepts and the objective identification of observable phenomena in terms of these concepts. What remains is the hypothetical aspect of the scientific procedure, which alone is described as "empirical" (whether confirmed by observation or not). This is a purely semantic proposition, empirically irrefutable. But the present writer sees no methodological advantage in accepting it.

Furthermore, with Pierce's definition of "empirical," his whole argument against Weber falls flat because Weber never claimed that *Verstehen* could be used as an experimental device. He presented and used it as an analytical procedure.

Weber defines human behavior as *action* "when and in so far as the acting individual attaches a subjective meaning to it."[9] A *social action* is an action "which in terms of its meaning, as intended by the actor or actors, is being related to the behavior of

others and thereby oriented in its course."[10] These propositions
are clearly what some logicians would call "nominal definitions"
whose test of validity lies not in an empirical verification but in the
applicability of the concept as an analytical tool, which, in turn is
determined primarily by its logical consistency with a theoretical
system. It is not the purpose of this paper to discuss the logical
consistency of Weber's theoretical system. However, as Weber
claims that his *verstehende Soziologie* is an *empirical* science, and
as this claim has been challenged, the crucial point here is whether
Weber's concept of "social action" is ultimately referable to human
perception, and whether *Verstehen* is a legitimate procedure for
the interpretation of the relevant data.

Verstehen clearly has reference to the *meaning* of an action
rather than to its form. The latter is directly observable to the sensory organs of sight, hearing, and touch; the former is not. How
do we know, then, that a meaning exists, and how can we identify
objectively the meaning of a specific action as intended by the actor? In other words, how do we *perceive* the subjectively intended
meaning of an action?

The answer is really quite simple:[11] We perceive the meaning
of an action in the same way as we perceive the meaning of a word
or a sentence (which, when spoken or written, is after all only one
specific type of social action). A whole series of inferences and
imputations are involved in this process. My immediate sense impression may be a series of vibrations of my eardrums which,
through a number of events in my nerve system, give the sensation
of a sequence of sounds varying in volume, pitch, and modulation.
My first inference may be that these sounds actually occurred at
the moment of time when I had my sensation. The next inference
is probably that these sounds as well as my sensation of them were
"caused" by corresponding events in the speech organs of an external object which, again through a number of inferences, I perceive as another person. Through a new series of inferences and
imputations, I perceive the sounds as symbols of ideas, attitudes,
volitions, or other mental conditions or processes which I recognize as adequately represented by the sounds I heard (that is, if I
had been in the other person's place and had perceived those ideas,
etc., as present in my own mind, I should possibly have uttered
similar sounds). I finally make the inference that these ideas, atti-

tudes, volitions, or other mental conditions or processes were actually present in the other person and that (for some reason which may be unknown to me) he intended to communicate that fact to me.

Of course, these inferences are not all made on the conscious level of thought. For the most part they are implied or taken for granted so that the mental process that we call "perception" seems to lead directly from the sensation of particular acoustic data called "sounds" to the percept of a "meaning" intended by the speaker.

It is an identical process that takes place in the perception of any action, verbal or non-verbal, whether I play the role of a direct respondent to the action or that of a passive observer. I perceive an action in terms of the actor's intention. If for some reason I cannot figure out what he intends to do, I have no way of knowing what he is actually doing, although I can observe certain motions of his body.

This, evidently, is what Weber refers to with the term *Verstehen*. It should be realized that the term does not necessarily imply the imputation of a specific *motivation* for a particular action. Weber is admittedly unclear on this point. But he does distinguish *aktuelles Verstehen* (understanding the meaning of an action) from *erklärendes Verstehen* (understanding the motivation —reason or purpose—of an action).[12] "Motivation" (*Zweck*) is something separate from the act and can only be "understood" in a broader situational context, while "meaning" (*Sinn*) is something inherent in the act itself, a "property" of the act rather than a "cause" or "purpose." Therefore, one can "understand" (*i.e.*, perceive) *what* a person is doing (in terms of his "intention") without knowing *why* he is doing it.

This is an important point because it refutes a misconception quite commonly held by critics of *Verstehen* as a scientific procedure, namely, that it should involve an *explanation* of observed phenomena in terms of their cause or motivation, or even the introduction of factual *information* beyond what is implied by the observed data.[13] As described and applied by Weber, the procedure of *Verstehen* may be compared to the perception of a simple object like, say, a ball. All I see is that half of the ball which is closest to me and which I perceive as an hemisphere. The other half I cannot see. But I do not hesitate to infer that it is there and that it has a form similar to the half that I see. I do not need the "information" of a mystical "sixth sense" to make this conclusion, nor do I, on the other hand, conclude that the assumed form of the invisible part is the "cause" that makes the visible part appear as an hemisphere. I have a partial sensation of a property (spheric form) that I recognize as the discriminating property of the concept "ball," and I immediately assume that the observed object really has that property. Likewise, I observe certain motions of the body of another person, motions that I immediately recognize as the visible part of an action of a particular intended meaning.

This leads us to the remaining question whether *Verstehen* in Weber's sense is a *legitimate* procedure in an empirical study of human behavior: Is the subjectively intended "meaning" of an action as well as its "form" ultimately referable to human perception?

To delve into the problems of an epistemological theory of perception would take us too far from our subject. A few points, however, must be mentioned. The first principle involved is what we may call the principle of *inference by analogy*. I observe the qualities A and B in conjunction in a number of cases. On the basis of this experience, A and B are associated in my mind, possibly to the extent that they are perceived as "properties" of an entity, C. Assuming a higher level of abstraction, we may say that I perceive an analogy between a number of sensations in which A and B are involved, and this perception of analogy is crystallized into a concept, C, which contains A and B as attributes. Once this association of percepts is established, I will infer the existence of C (with all its attributes) whenever I perceive either of the two qualities A or B. Perceiving A, I regard it as an adequate representation of C and thus infer, by analogy, the presence of B.

Undoubtedly, any inference by analogy is a source of error. I may be mistaken in any given instance. But the likelihood that I shall always be mistaken, or even most of the time, is very small. Therefore, I accept the inference as reasonably valid on the principle of *probability*. This is the second principle involved.

It should be noticed that the inference made in this case is not "conjured up" from nothing or from the fancy of pure imagination. The process is simply that the percepts obtained from immediate sensation of data are *complemented by percepts obtained from previous experience of similar data.* This is not only a legitimate procedure in empirical science but a necessary condition for the establishment of any scientific generalization.

Applying these principles to the concept of social action means that the immediate sensation of a person behaving in a particular manner is perceived as an observable "property" of a unit event, "social action," which also includes other properties, partly observable (*e.g.*, the respondent), partly inaccessible to immediate sensation (the state of mind of the actor). [14] The crucial question here, of course, is what kind of experience the observer has had, on the basis of which he can make the inference by analogy as to the presence or absence of a state of mind of the actor describable as a "subjectively intended meaning."

We could answer this question by simply referring to the fact that people act or behave either with or without "intention." This is undeniable on the basis of general human experience. It is even fairly easy to distinguish an intentional from an unintentional act. This, however, would be circumventing the crux of the question: How do we *know* when people act intentionally, and what their intentions are, since we can have no direct sensation of those intentions?

Reference was just made to "general human experience." The question is whether there is such a thing. That question must be answered in the affirmative. Were it not true, there could be no behavioral science. The conviction that it is true rests on the same *a priori* principle that is the foundation of all knowledge and all scientific endeavor, namely, that there is *order* in the universe. From this basic assumption several others are derived: (1) apparent similarities in our perception of the universe are true reflections of significant real similarities; (2) our conceptual classification of phenomena on the basis of these similarities is a true representation of real identities among observed objects, conditions, or events; (3) what is significantly true of one specimen as a member of a given class of phenomena is also true of the whole class as well as of each specimen within the class.

As these principles are applied to human behavior we get the following sequence:

> ... We note the likeness of the physical objects called other
> people's bodies to each other and to our own body; we also

note the likeness of their behaviour to our behaviour. In the case of our own behaviour, we can observe a number of correlations between stimulus and reaction (both being percepts). ... The behaviour of the percepts we call other people's bodies is similar to that of our own body in response to this or that stimulus; sometimes we experience the stimulus, but *suppose from their behaviour, that other people have experienced it....* [15]

In other words, from experience with my own person I know that my behavior "reflects" events in my nervous system, events that I perceive as ideas, emotions, intention, or volition. Observing another person's behavior, I infer by analogy that similar events are taking place in the other person's nervous system, that he perceives these events as ideas, emotions, intention, or volition, and that his behavior "reflects" these percepts.

The experience of *my own behavior*, then, is the ultimate source of my knowledge that human action has "meaning." And as my own experience is the only experience that I can ever perceive by direct sensation, it is ultimately the *only source* from which I can have empirical knowledge of even the existence (let alone the nature) of mental conditions and events in other persons. [16]

In making these inferences, I am still on solid empirical ground; as a matter of fact, I am on more solid ground than the physicist who, in order to describe the properties of light, conjures up "corpuscles" or "quanta"—or "waves"—which he can never hope to perceive by direct sensation, even through the finest of instruments. Yet physics is rightly regarded as the prototype of an empirical science.

Verstehen, however, implies more than the mere statement that action in general is associated with intended meaning. It means to identify the *specific* meaning of a *particular* action. This is what Weber refers to with the term *deutendes Verstehen,* which is only a fuller expression of what is implied in the shorter term.

Even here, according to Weber, inference by analogy from the observer's own experience is the most important source of interpretation. In this way, we may understand an action either rationally, as "when we attain a completely clear intellectual grasp of the action-elements in their intended context of meaning," or emotionally, as "when through sympathetic participation, we can adequately grasp the emotional context in which the action took place." [17]

There is an important qualification to this statement (frequently overlooked by Weber's critics): According to Weber, an action has to be "understandable" (*verstehbar*) in terms of established patterns of thought and behavior in order to be understood correctly. This is what Weber refers to with his term *Sinnadäquanz.* A "coherent course of conduct" is *sinnhaft adäquat,* i.e., adequate with respect to meaning, ". . . to the extent as the relationship between its parts is confirmed by us as a *typical* (we usually say: 'correct') context of meaning *according to the usual modes of thought and feeling.*"[18] Although Weber does not use the term "symbolic" in this connection, this is apparently what is implied. A social action, by its very nature of a *social* event (i.e., a communication from one person to another), implies a "meaning" as well as a "form." The latter serves, within the framework of a cultural situation, as a *symbol* by which the specific meaning of a particular action is conveyed from actor to respondent as well as (in a more or less voluntary manner) to the observer, provided he knows the "language." The "form" is the objective element of the complex phenomenon "action," which renders its "meaning" susceptible to perception.[19]

This should be sufficient to show that, correctly understood, the process of *Verstehen*, as described by Weber, not only meets all the requirements of a legitimate inference in empirical science, but is indispensable in the analysis of social phenomena. Moreover, it is a method which is widely used in all significant sociological research. Most explicit, and also most direct, is its use in participant observation; scholars who apply this technique are usually quite explicit in their concern about the interpretation ("meaning") of their data, and also aware of the problems and pitfalls involved.[20] But implicitly, the method of *Verstehen* is used by every student or research worker who applies an interview or a questionnaire. He uses the method in a more indirect way, adding another important source of error because the interviewer never comes near enough to the data he purports to study to make a single first-hand observation. Between the interviewer and the data is the testimony of the interview or the questionnaire —itself a "social action," the "intended meaning" of which can only be inferred through the process of *Verstehen*—provided it is *sinnhaft adäquat* and therefore *verstehbar* in terms of the symbolic patterns of the culture under study.

NOTES

1.   Albert Pierce, "Empiricism and the Social Sciences," *American Sociological Review,* 21 (April, 1956), pp. 135–137.

2.   *Ibid.,* p. 135.

3.   James B. Conant, *On Understanding Science,* New Haven: Yale University Press, 1947, p.48 (Mentor edition, New York: The New American Library, 1955, p.58).

4.   Pierce, *op. cit.,* p. 136.

5.   *Ibid.,* p. 137.

6.   *Ibid.,* p. 136.

7.   *Ibid.,* p. 136.

8.   *Ibid.,* p. 137.

9.   Max Weber, *The Theory of Social and Economic Organization* (translated by A. M. Henderson and Talcott Parsons), New York: Oxford University Press, 1947, p. 88.

10.   Max Weber, *Wirtschaft und Gesellschaft: Grundriss der verstehenden Soziologie* (4. edition, ed. Johannes Winckelmann), Tübingen : J. C. B. Mohr, 1956, p.1. We are here not following the translation by Henderson and Parsons (cf. *The Theory of Social and Economic Organization,* p. 88).

11.   The following draws extensively on Bertrand Russell, *The Analysis of Matter,* New York: Dover Publications, 1954, particularly chapter XX: "The Causal Theory of Perception," pp.197–217.

12.   *Wirtschaft und Gesellschaft,* pp. 3-4. The translation "direct observational understanding" for *aktuelles Verstehen (The Theory . . . , p. 94)* is not very satisfactory.

13.   See, e.g., Theodore Abel, "The Operation Called *Verstehen,*" *American Journal of Sociology,* 54 (November, 1948), pp. 211–218. Adler falls into a similar mistake when he charges that "*verstehende,* interpretive sociology aims at 'understanding,' a sort of aesthetic satisfaction in the student achieved by means of intuitional empathy" [Franz Adler, "The Value Concept in Sociology," *American Journal of Sociology,* 62 (November, 1956), p.275]. Again the confusion apparently stems from a failure to distinguish the analytical procedure of *verstehen,* which aims to determine the properties of an action in terms of its *Sinn,* from the hypothetical procedure of *erklären,* which aims to determine the functional

relationships of an action to preceding and following events in terms of its *Zweck.*

14.   Mead attempts to avoid having to "perceive" a subjective state of mind by describing the "meaning" of a gesture as "a development of something objectively there as a relation between certain phases of the social act..." but in the end identifies the "meaning" of an act with "the response of another organism" (George H. Mead, *Mind, Self and Society,* Chicago: University of Chicago Press, 1934, p.76, cf. p.145). Adler is more explicit: "The events probably preceding and following an action . . . are its meaning" and can be observed "without attempting to enter the actor's mind" (*op. cit.,* p. 277). The element of probability however, implies an expectation, *i.e.,* a "covert behavior" (or state of mind) on the part of the actor. Thus the basic difference between the "interpretive" and the "natural science" sociologist appears to be that the former knows that he is "attempting to enter the actor's mind," while the latter tries to uphold the illusion that he is not.

15.   Russell, *op. cit.,* p. 204 (emphasis added).

16.   Some will undoubtedly label this "introspection." That is purely a problem of description, and the name is no argument against the method, especially since it is not established how a person's perception of events and conditions in his own body is distinguishable from other experience. If it is introspection, let it be labeled so. It still remains the ultimate source of all empirical knowledge of the phenomenon called the human mind.

17.   *The Theory,* p. 91 (cf. *Wirtschaft und Gesellschaft,* p. 2).

18.   *Wirtschaft und Gesellschaft,* p. 5 (emphasis added). Henderson and Parsons erroneously attribute *"sinnhaft adäquat"* to "the subjective interpretation" of the course of conduct rather than to the conduct itself (*The Theory,* p. 99).

19.   Sorokin expresses exactly the same idea in the following terms: "Every process of meaningful human interaction consists of three components,... (1) thinking, acting, and reacting human beings as subjects of interaction; (2) meanings, values and norms for the sake of which the individuals interact, realizing and exchanging them in the course of interaction; (3) overt actions and material phenomena as vehicles or conductors *through which immaterial meanings, values, and norms are objectified and socialized.* [Pitirim A. Sorokin, *Society, Culture, and Personality,* New York: Harper & Bros., 1947, p. 41f. (italics added.]

20. See, e.g., Arthur J. Vidich, "Participant Observation and the Collection and Interpretation of Data," *American Journal of Sociology*, 60 (January, 1955), pp. 354-360.

5

On Misunderstanding
Verstehen: A Reply to Abel

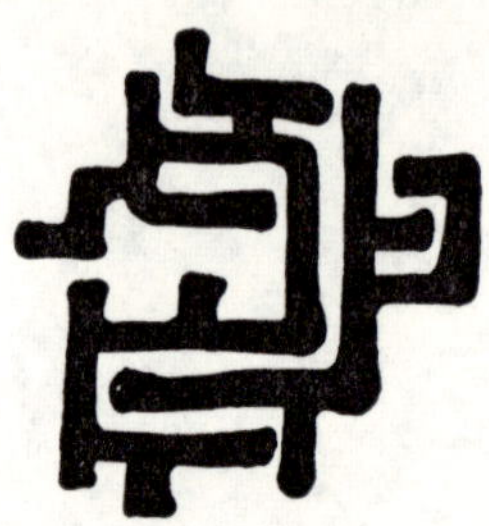

Murray L. Wax

In a direction very different from that of Munch, anthropologist
Murray L. Wax also argues that Abel's attack on *verstehen* is not
an operation or instrument to generate fresh knowledge or to
validate it, but is a precondition to research itself. Wax distinguishes four levels or varieties of *verstehen* and accuses Abel of
dealing with only one level of its meaning.

—MT

In an oft-cited essay,[1] Theodore Abel has analyzed critically "the
operation called Verstehen" and concluded that its limitations
virtually preclude its use as a scientific tool. Verstehen,[2] for him,
has value only as an ancillary to the activity of the social scientist.
Verstehen

> . . . relieves us of a sense of apprehension in connection with
> behavior that is unfamiliar or unexpected and it is a source of
> "hunches," which help us in the formulation of hypotheses.[3]

From *Sociology and Social Research* , *51* (April 1967), 323–333. Reprinted
by permission of the publisher.

The operation of Verstehen does not, however, add to our store of knowledge, because it consists of the application of knowledge already validated by personal experience; nor does it serve as a means of verification. The probability of a connection can be ascertained only by means of objective, experimental, and statistical tests.[4]

Yet, as Abel himself declares, "there is no dearth of tradition and authority behind the idea of Verstehen," and he mentions C. H. Cooley, P. Sorokin, R. M. MacIver, M. Weber, as well as Dilthey, Jaspers, and Rickert. For any sociologist thus to demolish or debunk a methodological procedure that was not only favored but purportedly used by such an international galaxy is truly a formidable achievement. To have done so in an essay of a brief ten pages is astonishing.

Given the quality of the protagonists of Verstehen, one is tempted to rebut Abel's essay pragmatically: for even if Verstehen were of no real value as a research procedure, surely belief in its efficacy has been one of science's more fruitful errors and certainly not to be condemned or discouraged. If a diet of Verstehen produced such an epochal work as *The Protestant Ethic and the Spirit of Capitalism,* then perhaps we should feed more of this illusionary meat to our contemporary students of society. To this rebuttal there is, of course, the counter that an error fruitful in one generation may prove sterile in the next. Still, I am inclined to wonder at the ease with which Abel disposed of so grand a host of antagonists. Could it be that we have here a classic case of the critique that overwhelms by ignoring the points at issue? I believe this is to be so and yet must qualify by recognizing that Abel can hardly be held responsible. So much confusion and ambiguity has enveloped this Germanic term that the critic has been free to select the meanings favorable to his own argument and prejudices.

If we turn for elucidation to Weber, whose essays on the Protestant ethic constitute one of the finest examples of verstehende historical sociology, we find theoretical concerns which have but little relation to the actual methodology of that aspect of this most famous of his works. The notes which constitute the introductory pages of *Wirtschaft und Gesellschaft*[5] purportedly address themselves to an analysis of Verstehen but instead transform the problem of understanding the meaning of an action into the specialized

problem of imputing motive to the actor. The same transformation
is repeated by Abel a generation later in the analysis of his first
"case" (shortly to be cited).[6] In thus restructuring the problem,
both men were responding not simply to the actual problems of
sociological and historical research where Verstehen was being employed, but to theoretical considerations of then contemporary
social-psychology where a main issue had been whether or not human nature should be regarded as motivated and, if so, whether or
not the imputation of motive could be a scientific procedure. For
present purposes, little would be gained by following further in
this social-psychological path or by adding further to the exegetical
literature on Weber. Instead, I shall attempt the more positive
function of explicating the possible meanings Verstehen might have
in social-scientific research while demonstrating how Abel has confused and distorted them.

I will be distinguishing four different levels or varieties of
understanding (insight, perception, explanation, etc.) that have
been or might be spoken of as Verstehen: first, extracultural
Verstehen; second, intracultural Verstehen; third, Verstehen as a
pattern analysis or interpretation; and fourth, Verstehen as interpersonal intuition. I shall argue that: the second is the most useful and appropriate meaning; the third would also be acceptable
but should be distinguished from the first; the first is of concern
to psychologists but not to sociologists; and the fourth is the product of a confusion imbedded in sociological tradition.

Under extracultural Verstehen would be included the "understanding" human beings have of the behavior of animals,[7] particularly
domesticated animals, which are spoken of as being playful, fright-
ened, hungry, angry, and the like. Conversely, pet animals are said
to "understand" their masters. While this kind of mutual "understanding" has been scoffed at by some psychologists, the accounts
of those researchers who have lived intimately with the higher apes
are especially convincing.[8] Also extracultural would be the understandings developed between persons of wholly alien cultures and
languages, from the simple inferences that one person might make
as to the elemental needs and feelings of the other to the more complex forms of transaction and understanding. However, these extracultural and extraspecies "understandings" belong more to the subject area of comparative psychology and would seem to be handled

adequately with such concepts as empathy and sympathy. Moreover, prolonged contact between persons of different cultures and languages will involve new socializations and the learning of languages or formation of symbol systems, and these processes bring us then to the second level of meaning for Verstehen.

Intracultural Verstehen could be approached from the context in which, a century ago, the Germanic term first acquired its specialized meaning—historical investigation.[9] However, our discussion will be more forceful if we think of ethnographic field research or, more simply, of the aural learning of a language. In all three of these cases, the student begins "outside" the interaction, confronting behaviors he finds bewildering and inexplicable: the actors are oriented to a world of meanings that the observer does not grasp. Thus, with a strange language, at first all is mumbo-jumbo, then patterns begin to emerge, and the student proceeds from halting discourse (stumbling over new phonemes and translating inwardly from his mother tongue) to the fluency of one increasingly at home in the language and situation. Likewise, the fieldworker finds initially that he does not understand the meanings of the actions of this strange people, and then gradually he comes to be able to categorize peoples (or relationships) and events: *e.g.* this man who is visiting as a brother-in-law to my host; last week his wife gave mine a gift; today he is expecting some reciprocity. Parallel illustrations might be drawn from historical investigation, where the student finds initially that, while he seems to be reading the text of a document, its meanings evade him, and then, later, as he gains familiarity with the historical period and the peoples involved, the same document speaks more profoundly.

The foregoing may be made clearer by a critical review of the first "case" presented by Abel in his attack on Verstehen:

> Last April 15 a freezing spell suddenly set in, causing a temperature drop from 60 to 34 degrees. I saw my neighbor rise from his desk by the window, walk to the woodshed, pick up an ax, and chop some wood. I then observed him carrying the wood into the house and placing it in the fireplace. After he had lighted the wood he sat down at his desk and resumed his daily task of writing.[10]

As Abel interprets it, someone applying "the operation of Verstehen" would conclude that "while working, my neighbor began to feel chilly and, in order to get warm, lighted a fire." But such a conclusion, he argues, "is obvious only because I have fitted the action of my neighbor into a sequential pattern by assuming that the stimulus 'drop in temperature' induced the response 'making a fire.' " In reality, we do not know that this stimulus-response relationship did in fact occur, and "the operation of Verstehen" has not yielded us any firm knowledge, useful in a scientific investigation.

Abel's critique is convincing because it has begged the question by misdirecting the Verstehen. The real Verstehen in this account has been completely overlooked, namely the recognition by the observer that the social objects involved were "neighbor," "desk," "ax," "woodshed," and so on, and that the actions were "chopping with an ax," "lighting (kindling) a fire," "writing (seated) at a desk," and so on. Abel, like much of the sociological audience that accepted his analysis, is accustomed to conducting his research within his own cultural milieu; so, he does not perceive the vast background of shared meanings assumed by the sophisticated (and quantitative) research techniques that he fancies, and accordingly, he speaks disparagingly of "knowledge derived from personal experience" as if this were a limitation rather than a foundation. Following the theoretical lead of Weber (cited above), he places the emphasis upon the imputation of motive which, and here he is quite correct, he sees as a difficulty in this kind of case, but he misses the point that the true level of Verstehen involved here is far deeper and more primitive. [11]

The notion that Verstehen should be considered an "operation" defines the situation incorrectly, as it implies that Verstehen should be a scientific instrument capable of generating fresh knowledge. Interpreted in the "intracultural" sense, Verstehen does not generate knowledge about a culture any more than being fluent in a language generates knowledge about it. Verstehen then is not an operation or instrument, it is a precondition of research. This is the more easily comprehended if we shift the emphasis from such incorrect uses as "applying the operation of Verstehen" and consider instead the acquisition of Verstehen, namely socialization, either the primary socialization into one's native culture, or the secondary socialization (or resocialization) into an alien culture, or—yet more tenuously—vicarious socialization.

Some readers may feel that I am weighing socialization too heavily, since it can, after all, be considered simply a form of "learning"; and, while they are prepared to grant that the researcher should learn something about a society before he begins his more detailed inquiries, yet the weight I am giving to Verstehen and socialization would seem more appropriate to a mystique or creed. One of the reasons for my procedure is that learning, as conceived by most psychologists, is a culturally static procedure (as the learning of nonsense syllables or mazes), whereas socialization implies participation in the cultural dynamic. Neither a culture nor a language can safely be regarded as a formal and static abstraction, as each is a dynamic system maintained and modified by its bearers or speakers. Because a language or dialect is created and defined by the continual dialog of its speakers, they are the only authority as to its nature, even though none of them may be able to perform a linguistic analysis of the language or delineate its phonemes or syntax. The same is true of culture, as it, too, is something borne and maintained and created by joint activity. Accordingly, the intracultural Verstehen deriving from primary socialization does yield a knowledge, or species of data, that is as absolute as any science. What native speakers say and respond to defines their dialect; what natives do, say, and respond to defines their culture.

Secondary socialization does not supply the field worker with the same authority as the native. However intimate and extensive an experience, no period of living within another culture can fully compensate for the lack of childhood experiences therein. Yet, because culture is a dynamic system maintained and modified by its members, participation is the most efficient way to gain as near a total grasp of it as is possible for the alien. In participating as he observes, the field worker undergoes a secondary socialization (or resocialization) which allows him to perceive the major categories of objects of the culture and to understand the major types of relationships and interactions. Thus, he gains something of an "insiders" view that it is extremely difficult to acquire with such secondary devices as structured questionnaires. In sociocultural anthropology, *The Andaman Islanders* and *The Argonauts of the*

Western Pacific both quickly assumed the stature of masterworks because they were the earliest studies based on prolonged and participating observation (with consequent resocialization). Thereafter, it became established that to acquire full status as an anthropologist, the student had to undertake a similarly intensive, participating field study, and, while this requirement does at times partake of a rite de passage, the rational, underlying justification is the experience of Verstehen which is thereby required.

In contrast, most U. S. sociologists have been focusing their research within their native country and upon research problems as specified by the authorities of middle-class society. As a result, these sociologists have but little awareness of the Verstehen upon which their activities has been based. [12] Moreover, in the investigation of these problems, these sociologists have relied upon sample survey procedures, and while the sample survey is a highly precise instrument for research within a culturally homogeneous society, it is a very blunt instrument for the perception and interpretation of cultural heterogeneity. For the sample survey is premised on the notion of a population that differs within itself only quantitatively (not qualitatively). And, just as educators who are saddled with a fixed curriculum have come to perceive of their balky pupils as a " culturally deprived" mass, so sociologists conducting sample surveys have come to see the mass of their respondents as being deficient, rather than as culturally different. [13] These sociologists are restricted by their research procedures to the most evident varieties of what I am terming intracultural Verstehen and, as a result, the reader of their reports seldom finds that via their pages he is encountering people who perceive the world differently than himself and the authors.

On the other hand, some sociologists have begun their investigations with the perception of cultural differences and have organized their research procedures accordingly, and where this has been done some excellent research has been produced, as on Plainville, Cantonville, and Cornerville, on opiate addicts, prisoners, high school pupils, and patients in mental asylums. In such investigations, the sociological researchers have undergone—as participating or semiparticipating observers—some degree of resocialization and been rewarded by a corresponding degree of Verstehen. Insofar as a target society was composed of adults recruited widely from the

national society (e.g. addicts, mental patients) the field worker has
not been handicapped by the lack of a corresponding childhood
socialization and has been limited in his participation only by
considerations of morality, legality, personal health, or time. Since
almost all of these subcultures are borne by societies in some sort
of conflict or (at the least) isolation from the "respectable middle-
class," the crucial problem of the field work experience has been
jumping the sociocultural "barrier" and acquiring the perspective of
the members.

The third level of meaning for Verstehen is as pattern analysis
and interpretation. Some sociocultural phenomena are such that
scholars have been able to analyze them as isolated systems and to
reduce them to, or toward, sets of formal patterns of principles;
the analysis of languages and of some kinship systems are the outstanding successes. In linguistic analysis perhaps it would be most
accurate to speak of the final result as an abstract system of patterns of patterns, which might imply that our analytic difficulties
with other cultural systems is the attempt at too simple a level of
abstraction. Be that as it may, the linguistic analysis has among
its properties that useful one of being complete, one key example
being that—within its vocal context—any elementary sound belongs
to one and only one phoneme class (or is not part of the dialect).
The formal, abstract, and logically complete analysis of language
is seldom, if ever, referred to under the category of Verstehen, but
partial analyses of other cultural phenomena as pattern systems are
sometimes so categorized. It is with the delineation of pattern in
historical societies that Verstehen is most often mentioned, although
if the concept makes sense on that interpretive level, it should be
applicable, not only to historical analysis, but to ethnological and
linguistic analysis—wherever there is the search for cultural patterning and the attempt to formalize the findings. Including linguistics under this rubric would have the desirable effect of setting
a standard toward which verstehende interpretations might proceed, or at least presenting a range of styles or possibilities of
interpretation. Linguistic analysis deserves from sociologists a
consideration as serious as it has been receiving from anthropologists as the kind of abstract model (competitive with classical mechanics and physics generally) that could be a goal for their
theories. [14]

Where the second and third levels of Verstehen harmonize is in their empirical focus upon the perspective of the actors themselves and upon the categories of distinctions which the actors recognize and respond to. By this I do not mean that the distinctions are always or ever clearly in the awareness of the actors.[15] (For example, the phonemic distinctions of language are operative outside of the awareness of the speaker, as are many of the other distinctions of social intercourse within a cultural milieu.) Socialization and participation are of such great importance in studying a group because thereby the field worker is forcibly made aware of the categories or distinctions—of experience and interaction— which are basic to the culture of the group although rarely the topic of their conversation. The analyses of language and of kinship systems are built upon this kind of field data, as they delineate and abstract the distinctive patterns underlying speech and action. In comparison, structural-functionalism tends the other way. As a mode of analysis employed by some students it is grounded in the categorical system of the society under study, but in the hands of many others of its students is a procedure they impose on the society, utilizing their theoretically-derived conceptions of the requirements of a social system. This latter variety of structural-functionalist sees formal and insightful analyses as counterposed to each other, because insight in its sociological sense is the recognition of an implicit pattern. However, what is being argued here is that insight and understanding can characterize certain kinds of formal systems, namely those based on the delineation and abstraction of pattern.

Earlier in this paper, I referred to *The Protestant Ethic and the Spirit of Capitalism* as an outstanding example of verstehende historical sociology. Some sociological theorists have scorned the intellectual attention given to this among the works of Weber, preferring to see his greatness in his more architectonic (and less verstehende) structures. In like manner, some of the musicological elite have deplored the attention given the choral works of J. S. Bach, preferring to see his greatness in the architectonic *Art of the Fugue*. In both cases I suspect the experts of overpraising the abstruse in order to defend their elite status against the claims of the less erudite. While Weber's comparisons and generalizations among civilized societies do constitute an impressive piece of scholarship and a brave attempt at formalization, his understanding of non-Western societies was much less profound than it was of the Protestant sectarians. What Weber communicates in *The Protestant Ethic and the Spirit of Capitalism* is much more than a record of events and more even than the functional consequences of changes in religious ethos, it is an insightful portrait of how a people so alien to his and our contemporary spirit defined their world and their activities within it. So the reader comes to understand how the strictest sectarian piety could lead to that rational and diligent business enterprise which meant for the individual the amassing of wealth and for society at large the development of rational bourgeois capitalism. [16]

Discussion of Verstehen as interpersonal intuition (or inter-subjective understanding including the imputation of motive) has been postponed until this late point in the paper because I take this level of meaning to be incorrect. Cooley, Weber, and others in their theoretical discussions have regarded Verstehen as if it did represent a kind of knowing or understanding which one individual might have of another (and to be differentiated from the kind of knowing the scientists might gain of the atom). By failing to specify the cultural context of this process of knowing, they provided the grounds for the critique of Abel, who argued that, in effect, Verstehen was a kind of intuitive or informal species of psychological knowledge:

> . . . the operation of Verstehen involves three steps: (1) internalizing the stimulus, (2) internalizing the response, and (3) applying behavior maxims. . . .
>
> Behavior maxims are not recorded in any textbooks on human behavior . . . they are generalizations of direct personal experience derived from introspection and self-observation. [17]

And since, as Abel views man, he is poor in his psychological insight, Verstehen is a dubious procedure for science.

If, however, we place our observer and interpreter in his culture and in his roles, then Abel's critique becomes irrelevant. The individual understands and knows what those who participate in that culture and play those roles have to understand and know, and this includes the ability to interpret the conduct of those whose roles are complementary.

In a society, such as ours, where the imputation of motive is
a significant aspect of role-playing, individuals will develop appropriate and useful vocabularies for imputing motives to others and
to themselves; some may even read "textbooks on human behavior"
to develop more formidable or convincing vocabularies of motive
or styles of imputation. But if Verstehen is interpreted as the
imputing of motive, then it will have no relationship to the historical or ethnographic research where the concept truly applies.

NOTES

1.   An earlier draft of this paper was delivered at the 1965 annual
meetings of the Midwest Sociological Society, where it received the
benefit of comments by Bennett M. Berger. The paper was then
revised and delivered in its present form at the 1966 annual meetings
of the American Sociological Association.
Since the term "Verstehen" is naturalized among American
sociologists, I will not hereafter in this article italicize it as if it
were a foreign word, but treat it as a proper noun.

2. "The Operation Called *Verstehen*," *Readings in the Philosophy of Science*, ed. Herbert Feigl and May Brodbeck (New York:
Appleton-Century-Crofts, 1953), 677–87, reprinted from *American
Journal of Sociology*, 54 (1948).
At the time when I first drafted this essay, the one major
attempt at rebuttal that I knew of was Peter A. Munch, "Empirical
Science and Max Weber's *Verstehend Soziologie*," *American Sociological Review*, 22 (February, 1957), 32–38. As we shall be noting
below, some of Munch's argument is helpful. However, on the
whole it is beclouded by a preoccupation with an epistemology
that is naively empiricist (concerning which see the criticism of
C. West Churchman in *Theory of Experimental Inference* (New
York: The Macmillan Co., 1958), Chap. 6. Perhaps because of
this defect, Munch's rebuttal does not seem to have affected the
flow of citations of approval to Abel's article even by such otherwise sophisticated author as Abraham Kaplan (cf. *The Conduct of
Inquiry* (San Francisco: Chandler Publishing Co., 1964), 141 f.).
More recently, I have encountered Peter Winch's *The Idea
of a Social Science* (London: Routledge & Kegan Paul, 1958), which
contains a brilliant and succinct exposition of the point of view I
adopt in this essay but which does not deal with Abel's essay. The
interested reader is referred to chapter four of Winch's book.

With the more recent "Max Weber's *Verstehen*," William T.
Tucker, *The Sociological Quarterly, 6* (Spring, 1965), 157–65, I
find more agreement than with Munch, but less than with Winch,
and I shall be referring to specific areas as I go along. My most important disagreement is with his acceptance of the interior/exterior
dichotomy that has so bedeviled psychology.

3. *Loc. cit.*, 686–87.

4. *Ibid.*, 687.

5. Translated into English by A. M. Henderson and T. Parsons as
section I. 1a of *The Theory of Social and Economic Organization*
(New York: The Free Press, a Division of the Macmillan Co., 1947),
89–112.

6. One of the virtues of Munch's article is that he does perceive
that the issue is one of meaning and the perception of action as
meaningful. He also recognizes that "We perceive the meaning of
an action in the same way that we perceive meaning of a word or
sentence" (p. 28), but then he loses his way amid epistemology.
Tucker likewise sees that the issue is one of meaningful behavior,
but straddles the issue by declaring that "Intentional behavior,
meaningful behavior, and subjectively understandable behavior are,
all three synonymous with regard to *Verstehen*" (*loc. cit.*, 157–58).
He believes that he escapes from the problems inherent in imputing
motive by speaking of "socially generated motivations." However,
C. Wright Mills' famous paper on "Situated Actions and Vocabularies of Motive" should make the researcher leary of any procedure
involving the imputing of motive. And, from an anthropological
perspective, there is the fact that many folk peoples are uncon-
cerned with intentions and do not impute motives to actors, and
yet, nonetheless, such folk do regard actions as meaningful [cf. the
essays of Dorothy D. Lee in *Freedom and Culture* (Englewood
Cliffs, N. J.: Spectrum Books, 1959)].

7. Cf. M. Weber, *op. cit.*, 104.

8. Cf. Konrad Z. Lorenz, *King Solomon's Ring* (New York: Apollo
Editions—A-16, Thomas Y. Crowell, 1961); Cathy Hayes, *The Ape
in Our House* (New York: Harper & Bros., 1951); Wolfgang Köh-
ler, *The Mentality of Apes* (New York: Harcourt Brace and Co.,
1926).

9. Cf. Winch, *op. cit.*, 88f., 131f. In these arguments, Winch in
turn cites R. G. Collingwood's *The Idea of History*.

10.   *Loc. cit.,* 679

11.   Tucker makes the same error in interpreting this case as does Abel, for he argues that the case is not germane "since Abel's hypothetical situation is non-social," while Weber's scheme is designed to explain social action" (*loc. cit.,* 164–65).

12.   Again, one of the virtues of Munch's article is that he perceives closeness of connection between Verstehen and participant observation while also recognizing that "implicitly, the method of Verstehen is used by every student or research worker who applies an interview or a questionnaire" (p. 32).

13.   Leopold J. Shapiro. "The Opinion Poll," unpublished Ph.D. dissertation, Department of Sociology, University of Chicago, 1956; David Riesman and Mark Benney, "The Sociology of the Interview," *Midwest Sociologist* 18 (1956), 3–15.

14.   The interest of sociocultural anthropologists in linguistic-type formalizations and models is of some age. In recent years the interest has become much more concentrated and has issued in a variety of proposals and programs (e.g. Claude Levi-Strauss, Ward Goodenough). See also Murray Wax, "The Tree of Social Knowledge," *Psychiatry* 28 (May, 1965), 99–106.

15.   The classic and still best reference is Edward Sapir, "The Unconscious Patterning of Behavior in Society," (1927) reprinted in *Selected Writings of Edward Sapir,* ed. David Mandelbaum (Berkeley: University of California, 1949), 544–59. See also such more recent and particular studies as those of Edward Hall, *The Silent Language.*

16.   I am pleased to discover that in a paper written in 1964 for use in the social-science curriculum of Montieth College, R. H. Wright has formulated a similar interpretation of *The Protestant Ethic and the Spirit of Capitalism.* Wright argues that this work is a pattern analysis akin to that of anthropologists, such as Sapir, R. Benedict, and D. D. Lee, and explains that "pattern analysis is an attempt to locate certain kinds of definitions—pervasive assumptions—from the behavior of persons who belong to a particular cultural unit" ("Towards a Phenomenology of Social Class," Montieth College, October, 1964).

17.   *Loc. cit.,* 682–84.

6

A Reply to Professor Wax

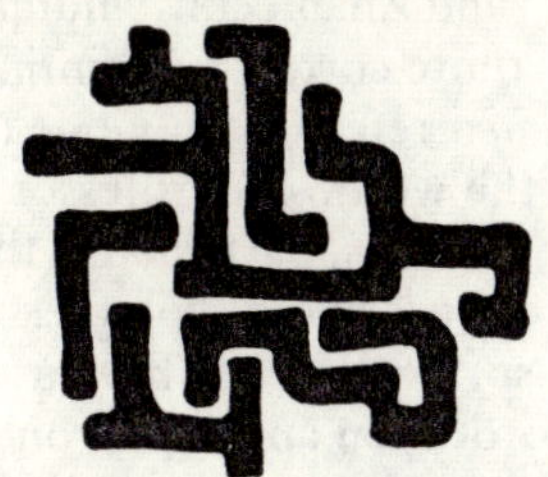

Theodore Abel

Abel responds to Wax indicating that he would agree with Wax's discriminations but that they are largely beside the point. The issue is by no means closed, and the literature on this problem continues.[1] But the problem has growingly been a concern with incorporating *verstehen* into a naturalistic model for the social sciences rather than a continued concern with differentiating the social from the natural sciences, at least in this second phase of the debate.

—MT

NOTE

1. For other recent pieces in the debate among sociologists, see: Baar (1967), Braude (1966), Bruyn (1966), George (1969), Marquis (1968), Stewart (1971), Tucker (1965), and Winthrop (1964).

I. ON THE USE OF THE TERM 'VERSTEHEN'

In his excellent paper Professor Wax discusses the variety of meanings of the term *verstehen* in the German language. The

From *Sociology and Social Research*, *51* (1967), 334–336. Reprinted by permission of the publisher.

equivalent term in English, *understanding*, has an equally rich variety of meanings. Both terms refer to the act of comprehending the subjective or mental factors involved in human behavior, such as meaning, insight, evaluation, motive, attitude, Thomas' "definition of the situation," and Znaniecki's "humanistic coefficient."

Professor Wax is quite correct in pointing out that what I have said about *verstehen* refers to only one of several linguistically possible uses of the word. As Professor Wax says, I did not consider its other applications, particularly the important role it plays in the study of culture and of complex historical phenomena. Had I intended to do so, I would not have used the term *verstehen*. Why use a German word when an English one would do as well?

Professor Wax seems to have overlooked the fact that *verstehen* is used by sociologists in a special sense and for special reasons. When they speak of *verstehen* they do not have all the connotations of the word in the German language in mind. Among sociologists, *verstehen* has become a technical term for motivational analysis, a usage that derives directly from Max Weber.

As far as I know, the term first appeared in American sociological literature in my book *Systematic Sociology in Germany*.[1] I used "Verstehende Soziologie" in the heading of my chapter on Weber. The phrase accurately describes Weber's sociological position for he defined sociology as the study of social actions and postulated that they cannot be explained causally without knowledge of the subjective intentions of the actors. I believe that the term *verstehen* was incorporated into the sociological vocabulary because it obviated the necessity for coining a neologism to stand for such more or less cumbersome phrases as: "subjective interpretation of meaning," "motivational understanding," "comprehension of intent," "valuational intention syndrome." The very frequent reference to Max Weber's writings by American sociologists also fostered the use of the word *verstehen*. As Parsons rightly observed: "it has not seemed advisable to attempt a rigorous use of a single English term whenever Weber employs Verstehen."[2]

It is true that the four different levels of understanding described by Professor Wax "have been or might be spoken of as Verstehen." But they are not so spoken of by sociologists. Even German scholars tend to limit the use of the word to Weber's meaning. For example, the kind of *understanding* or *verstehen* which is provided by what Professor Wax calls "pattern analysis" and Sorokin calls "the logico-meaningful method," German scholars designate by the term *hermeneutics* (from Hermes, the Interpreter).

The restriction of the term *verstehen* to one of its many meanings is, of course, an arbitrary convention. But the selection was not made by Weber, or anyone else, "because it is favorable to argument and prejudices," as Professor Wax seems to imply, but because it is useful and efficient. It should also be clear that in dealing with the operation connected with *verstehen* as a technical sociological term I have not "confused and distorted the possible meanings of Verstehen," I have intended to refer to only one of these.

II. ON THE USEFULNESS OF THE CONCEPT 'VERSTEHEN'

Professor Wax interprets an article as an attack on *verstehen* and claims that I have "demolished and debunked a methodological procedure" that has the support of many distinguished scholars. An even stronger accusation was made by a Dutch sociologist who stated that: "Abel has interred the operation called verstehen once and for all with a funeral oration."[3]

Nothing can be further from my intent. I fully share Weber's view that the understanding of subjective factors in the study of social behavior is necessary and indispensable. It was precisely for this reason that I set out to examine the process by which we conduct motivational analysis. I wanted to make the use of the operational concept of *verstehen* as efficient and effective as possible.

In the course of my analysis I came up with several findings about what we do when we try to understand human conduct motivationally. In my opinion, the most important finding pertains to the observation, among others, that in the use of *verstehen* we employ general rules of a specific kind by means of which we establish connections between observed behavior and the conditions that evoke it. I have called these general rules *behavior maxims*. In the explanation of human behavior they play a role similar to the role assigned to laws in the logical model of explanation developed by Hempel and Oppenheim.[4]

I certainly do not hold the opinion, attributed to me by Professor Wax, that the operation of *verstehen* is only an "ancillary" tool for sociological analysis. On the contrary, in my opinion *verstehen* is the chief source of hypotheses in sociology. It is an indispensable tool for the study of social behavior. The fact that the operation which generates hypotheses cannot itself be used to verify or falsify them does not detract from its significance.

In summing up my article I wrote: The operation of *verstehen* does not add to our store of knowledge. I think that this statement is the main reason why its critics have regarded the article as a "funeral oration" and I have lived to regret it!

What I had in mind is the fact that since *verstehen* (as motivational understanding) is confirmed by generalizations based on direct personal experience (behavior maxims), it does not itself lead to the formulation of new *behavior maxims*. I did not intend to say that *verstehen* cannot lead to other kinds of knowledge, such as the disclosure of connections between social phenomena and other insights. Indeed, my interest in Weber's concept *verstehen* stems from my conviction that it is an important tool for the explanation of knowledge in the social sciences.

NOTES

1. Theodore Abel, *Systematic Sociology in Germany*, Second Edition (New York: Octagon Books, 1966).

2. Max Weber, *The Theory of Social and Economic Organization* (New York: Oxford University Press, 1947), note pp. 87–88.

3. R. F. Berling (Leiden), in a paper presented on January 1964 at a meeting of the Netherlands Sociological Society in commemoration of Weber's 100th anniversary.

4. G. G. Hempel, and P. Oppenheim, "Studies in the Logic of Explanation," *Philosophy of Science*, 15 (1948).

7

Social Action, Behavior and *Verstehen*

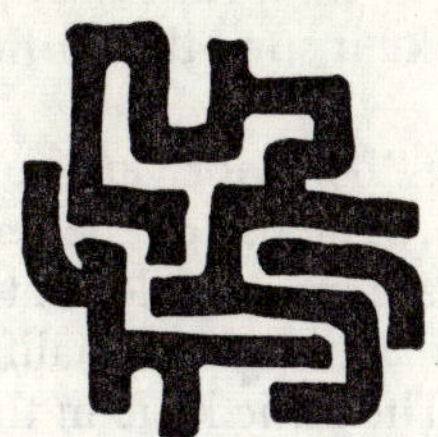

Charles K. Warriner

Following a position similar to that of Wax, Charles K. Warriner here extends the argument for the proper use of *verstehen* as a "descriptive catalog" of meanings used by the actors under examination, especially the field worker. Through the externalization of that listing, Warriner argues, we can separate *verstehen* as an *inference* from its uses as an *observation* of meanings. The question the behaviorist would ask, however, might be: If one *fully* externalizes *verstehen*, one is talking about behaviors of the actors, so why complicate the dialogue by speaking of meanings at all? [1]

—MT

NOTE

1. A similar debate rages between phenomenological and behavioristic orientations in psychology, wherein the philosophic issues have been dealt with in a far more sophisticated manner than in sociology, which could probably profit from that exchange (e.g., see Wann, 1964).

From *The Sociological Quarterly*, *10* (1969), 501–511. Reprinted by permission of the publisher. This is a revised version of a paper read at the 30th Annual Meeting of the Midwest Sociological Society, Madison, Wisconsin, April 22, 1966.

Ever since Watson fixed the meaning of the term "behavior" in a neuromuscular context, there have been reactions to its use in sociology. At times these reactions emerge as explicit disavowals of the appropriateness of the term in a sociological vocabulary, but often it is reluctantly used with a variety of proscriptive and definitional statements that make it something other than what Watson had in mind.

These problems with "behavior" are not merely matters of terminological preference. The use of the term often involves a set of commitments that are methodological and metaphysical as well as substantive. The reactions and qualifications have to do with these orientations. The basic issue in this controversy is whether the scientific observation of human action can encompass *meaning* or whether all observation of action reduces to the observation of neuromuscular movement in space and time. In this latter case meaning does not exist as a scientifically comprehensible fact or else it is an inference from or extrapolation of relations among these basic facts.

This problem of the role and nature of meaning in scientific observation of human phenomena periodically recurs in every specialty in the social sciences. For example, in recent years the development of componential analysis in ethnology has again raised the issue in linguistics. As recently as 1962, Hill asserted that the "investigation of sound is our only avenue to knowledge of the mental linguistic substances." Chafe (1965:23), quoting Hill, then says: "My own view is rather at the other extreme: that meaning is in every way as important as sound in our approach to an understanding of language as a whole."

The behaviorist treatment of this issue is a special case because Watson's position on meaning became confused with the more general methodological directive to pay attention to that which is observable. The emphasis upon the necessity for following scientific canons was intermingled with a much more particular prescription and judgment about what was observable. This confusion was sustained by the assumption that physical facts have a greater reality than others and by the belief that objective observation could be based only on naive sense perception. Within this frame of thought, the use of the term behavior implies the judgment that neuromuscular behavior is the fundamental and intrinsic unit of action and the only unit of observation.[1] All other units of analysis—interaction, social action, conduct—consist of combinations of units of behavior and are explicable and observable only in terms of these "more basic" units.

Despite the heavy weight of the arguments against including meaning in scientific concerns, sociologists and anthropologists have often gone right ahead observing social actions in units that are defined by their meaning. Unfortunately, theory and concepts are much more responsive to these *a priori* arguments than is research so that there is often a kind of sociological "schizophrenia" in which we theorize in terms of behavior, but do our research in terms of social conduct. As a result, there are often inane procedural proposals which stem from our need to assure ourselves of scientific objectivity.[2]

The social scientist does and must deal with "saluting a flag," "going to church," "arguing," "teaching a class," "sawing a board," "playing bridge," "praying," "voting," and "buying a dress." Generally, in practice the sociological field worker does observe these kinds of acts, and he does so without reference to the neuromuscular criteria of the behaviorist. These are not "behaviors" in the Watsonian sense. These are units of action with their own character, consequences, and connections which we do and must observe if we are to study groups, associations, and societies. It is the conceptual nature of these units and the justification of the method of their observation that has been the problem, not their relevance or importance.

The purpose of this paper is the specification of the criteria for these units of social conduct and an analysis of the operations by which scientific observation of such meaningful units is made. I hope thereby to strengthen the position of those who have opposed the use of behavior as the fundamental theoretical and empirical unit and in the process to add a bit to the clarification of the relation of *verstehen* to empirical sociological research.

In sociology, the attempts to deal with action in units different from neuromuscular behavior have come from two major sources. There were others, of course, but it is the disciples of George Herbert Mead and of Max Weber who have been most centrally involved in the objections to "behavior" and who have attempted to bring meaning into our concerns with action.

Max Weber attempted to deal with what he saw as the uniquely human characteristic of meaning by treating it as the "orientation" or "intent" of the actor in action. Thus, meaning was an additional fact, related to, but not intrinsically a part of, action units. For Weber, action was behavior that was meaningful, social action was action, i.e., meaningful behavior that was oriented toward others. Since meaning is an additional fact added to behavior, the issue of behavior as a unit of action is not crucial for Weber and his followers. (Hence Parsons, for example, uses the term behavior without difficulty.) *Verstehen* was proposed as the methodology for getting at these meanings rather than as a method for the observation of action itself. As I shall show later, certain of Weber's ideas about *verstehen* as an operation and his conception of meaning may be construed in quite a different way such that his position is a more direct challenge to the behaviorist definition of action than it has appeared to be.

Mead's concern with action as gestures in the interactional process is the second major source of objections to the use of "behavior." Mead viewed the external, observable act as being structured by and in terms of the problem of communication to self and to others. This point of view involves a much more explicit rejection of "behavior" for concern is focused upon the gesture as a mark of meaning. Hence "behavior" as neuromuscular units of action is an irrelevancy. In this view the unit of action for observation and analysis is the linguistic sign, the word or the gesture, that means something to the participants. The neuromuscular aspects of gestures and the physical production of language signs are taken as given, and attention is directed toward the organization of these into sign units which are recognizable to self and others as units. However, because of their preoccupation with language and with communication, the followers of Mead have failed to come to grips with the basic problem of the units of observation to be used for the activity of humans that is not primarily linguistic or gesturally symbolic.

From a sociological perspective, what human actors do is defined and organized by their conceptions of what an act, any particular act, is. The actors in a society structure their activity into unit acts which are recognized by themselves and others as units. That is, complex trains of neuromuscular and skeletal movements, involving many kinds of chemical and physiological processes, are identified by the participants as unit acts, named and recognized as totalities. This recognition and naming occurs even though there may be rather wide variations in the neuromuscular aspects of the performance.

What is most immediately apparent about this structuring is that it is collective, consensual, and conventional. The actors in any particular group "understand," i.e. recognize, what these acts are, what they contain, what they include, just as the reader "understands" them merely by a recitation of their names.

Most of these illustrations are of unit acts that are widely recognized in American society, but certain acts within the society, especially in subgroups are meaningless to the stranger. Although he could record movements in space and time, identify muscles and nerves, he would have no way of identifying the units of activity, of isolating the units in terms of which that set of actors was acting. This fact becomes especially apparent whenever we go into a society with quite different conventional understandings than those with which we are familiar. At first we need an informant handy to answer our question, "What is going on now?" Otherwise, with Herman Melville (1923:193), we must report that in their actions they appear ". . . like a parcel of 'Freemasons' making secret signs to each other. I was everything, but could comprehend nothing."

Thus, the basic observational problem for the sociologist is to be able to identify in the ongoing society those units of action which are recognized by the members of the society we are studying and in terms of which their activity is structured. This is what Becker and Geer (1957) refer to as "learning the native language." This requires that we first obtain an understanding of the action language of the participants. When we do this, as Warner (1959: 480) says, our "own carefully developed meanings are also a part of (our) evidence."

Becker and Geer's use of "learning the native language" in talking about social action is not simply metaphorical. The problem here is identical to the problem facing the linguist who must learn the phonemic structure of each language if he is to study that language even at the phoneme level. In fact, I would argue that language is a specialized sub-category of social action and that we are faced with problems identical to those of the linguist.

It is at this point that the epistemological and methodological issues are raised that make the field worker uncomfortable and that cause the theorist to revert to the term "behavior." If we are to observe the directives for a natural science of society, how can we have objective, empirical observation when the units of observation are defined in terms of their "meanings" to the participants, and the research procedure depends upon the "meanings" held by the observer, "carefully developed" or not? Are we not right back to the very position which behaviorism as a methodology was designed to overcome? Are we not back to the technique of *verstehen* as it has been so fully criticized on subjectivist and mentalistic grounds?

This statement of the problem involves several confusions. The issues arise because we have not been clear about what it is in fact that a good field worker does in the observation of action. We have not been clear because (1) we have confused the problem of actor motivation with meaning, and because (2) we have assumed that in every case "meaning" meant what the actor has in his mind at the time of the action. As I shall show, this is not what Warner implies by "carefully developed meanings," nor, perhaps, what Weber meant by "intent."

That these confusions can be avoided is demonstrated by the development of componential analysis in ethnology. This method for the observation of cultural phenomena in meaningful terms had its origins in structural linguistics, and is concerned with the same basic problem as the meaningful analysis of action in sociology.

> Componential analysis is useful precisely insofar as it explicates the fundamental cultural categories. . . .The question with which compenential analysis deals is precisely that of native categories as cultural categories. . . . (Schneider, 1965: 289)

In the development of componential analysis, one of the basic problems has been the specification of the implicit dimensions that "natives" use in ordering their (linguistic) conduct. Many of the techniques and procedures for the componential analysis of language could and should be applied to the analysis of action systems (e.g., the technological action system in a factory and the relational action system in sociability clubs).

However, this approach takes as given that language can be described in semantic units and that we need not restrict ourselves to phonology. Chafe (1965) does demonstrate that semantic units and phonemic units are not identical, but there is generally little concern with the question of how we observe the semantic units. It is clear, however, that this approach, starting with cultural conceptions, has not been confused by the question of actor motivation, nor by the problem of what the actor now has in his mind. The fact of cultural understandings or collective representations is accepted.

A social act as a structural unit does not depend upon actor motivation or other characteristics. "Sawing a board" as a unit social act exists as an identifiable fact regardless of the unique end in view (whether it is getting a wage or constructing a tree house, dog house, or toy house), regardless of the internal state of the actor (his emotions), and regardless of his physiology, handedness, musculature, or effectiveness. Others watching can identify the act regardless of variations in these dimensions. There are times when variations in these other characteristics may be important because of our particular research problem, but these are additional facts to be observed.

The problem then is simply that of how we observe action units defined by the collective representations of the actors, and how this observation can be given scientific legitimacy as an objective and reliable procedure that does not involve insight, inference, or some other mystical connection between the world of events and the recordings of the observer.

Ideal observation occurs in those situations where the observer is required to make only simple sensory discriminations. Reliability and objectivity are highest when the observer is asked only to distinguish black from white, or even more simply, to distinguish between a pointer at this line (on a wave-length scale, for example) from one at that line. Observation of this sort is an ideal rarely achieved except as it is preceded by a long history of observation requiring much more complex judgments and more elaborate discriminations on the part of the observer.

The variation in the complexity of the judgments required of the observer does not basically involve the question of objectivity. It is rather the question of reliability. Distinguishing red from black can be just as objective, though a less reliable procedure, than reading the position of a pointer on a spectographic scale. Objectivity is determined by the extent to which there are criteria for judgment. Objectivity requires a *standard*, whether a scale, a prototype model, a color card, or a list of descriptive statements against which the thing or event observed can be compared in order to judge whether it is or is not congruent.

In many cases in the physical and biological sciences, as well as in the social sciences, the standard for judgment is so complex that it cannot be easily given as a scale, a prototype, or a list. In these cases the observer learns the criteria for judgment in his training and it becomes a part of his mental equipment and his personal professional skill. Thus, to see a pi-meson in a photographic plate of a cloud chamber involves a complex standard which the physicist has learned in his training. Hanson (1965) reflects this when he says that "the visitor must learn at least some physics before he can see what the physicist sees." That it is an external, though not externalized, objective standard is demonstrated by inter-observer reliability.

The trouble with *verstehen*, as it is often understood, with sympathetic introspection, and with taking the role of the other is that they had no objective standard in terms of which judgments were made, and no standard was thought possible or necessary because it was assumed that the crucial process was inference rather than judgment.

On the other hand, the procedure implied by Warner's "carefully developed meanings" is quite different. Warner implies that what the field worker does is to develop a descriptive catalog of acts such that at any moment in time he can compare what is being done with the previously developed descriptions and make the judgment that the observed event is or is not the same as that in the catalog.

The implication of the emphasis Warner places on the development of the scale is that to be useful and productive for sociology, the descriptions must come from the conventional understandings in the society observed—i.e., they must be culturally valid. (These understandings may differ from time to time and from group to group so that the observer needs a different set of descriptions for one series of observations than for another, but this does not detract from the objectivity of the method as long as the descriptions are prepared prior to the observations which are to be used as data.)

In terms of the basic methodological procedure, these descriptions could come from any source and be based on any criteria—physical, physiological, or social. The method consists simply of comparing the observed event with the list, catalog, scale, or protocol and making the judgment that they do or do not correspond. For physiological purposes the criteria are neuromuscular ones, for technological purposes they are physical ones, for sociological purposes the criterion is that of "native" structuring.

We have failed to recognize that this is the procedure in good sociological field work because the descriptive list has seldom been systematically *externalized*. Because of the complexity of the descriptions, the standard has been a part of the training of the field worker, and thus a part of his professional skill rather than an explicitly written description. At the present time we have no technique as efficient and effective as the trained observer to carry the lengthy list of acts and their descriptions in such a way that all items are immediately available and to make the instantaneous sortings on the basis of complex criteria that are required by the nature of the phenomena. The problem of instrumentation is like, but more complex than that of teaching machines to read handwriting. The wide range of variation in a handwritten word, easily and quickly identifiable by a human observer is still too difficult for a machine.

This same procedure is used in everyday life for the interpretation of the *content* of gestures, for getting at the messages of what people say or do, and this same procedure is used by good interviewers. The signs presented, whether a gesture or a linguistic sign, are compared against a "dictionary" that we carry in our heads—a description of the *previously* agreed upon referents of the sign. The difference between the scientific and lay uses of this procedure is only that the scientist takes more care in the development of his "dictionary" and in the specification of the situations for which it is valid.

There is some indication that Weber had this procedure in mind in his discussion of *verstehen,* but he did not clearly separate the observation of action or of meaning in this sense from the different operation, the *inference* that the meaning identified by the dictionary is now in the mind of the actor. For this reason there is confusion as to Weber's reference when he speaks of "intent." Munch (1957:29) asserts that Weber distinguished motivation from intent or orientation of the act:

> Motivation (*Zweck*) is something separate from the act and can only be understood in a broader situational context, while meaning (*Sinn*) is something inherent in the act itself, a property of the act rather than a cause or purpose. Therefore, one can understand (i.e., perceive) *what* a person is doing (in terms of his intention) without knowing *why* he is doing it.

Munch (1957:12,13) goes on to assert that the process of observation "is simply that the percepts obtained from immediate sensation of data are complemented by percepts obtained from previous experience of similar data," and notes that according to Weber, "an action has to be 'understandable' (*verstehbar*) in terms of established patterns of thought and behavior."

In his excellent paper on *Verstehen*, Murray Wax (1967:329) clearly makes this point. He criticizes Abel for focusing on the imputation of motive and distinguishes this interpretation of *Verstehen* from its use as "an empirical focus upon the perspective of the actors themselves and upon the categories of distinctions which the actors recognize and respond to." In this connection, Wax (1967:327) points out that the "secondary socialization" (resocialization) of the observer is of prime significance whether in studying one's own society or another for it is this resocialization that "allows him to perceive the major categories of objects in the culture.

It appears that in this conception of *Verstehen* there are present all of the elements necessary to the objective observation of action. However, none of the commentators distinguish the preparation for observation (the resocialization) from the act of observation itself.

But, from the point of view of the logic, and hence the justification of the method, we must clearly recognize that the important observational act is a *judgment*, a judgment that what is seen is or is not the same as is described in the *previously developed descriptive standard*, dictionary or catalog.

It is possible to say that "meaning" is a "property of the act" as Weber does, only if "meaning" refers *exclusively* to this pre-

viously developed descriptive catalog of acts that is the framework
by which the observer sees the act. Meaning is then a property of
the act in a very real sense, but so would be any judgmental criteria from whatever source! When Munch speaks of "percepts obtained from experience with similar data," he is clearly referring
to the same thing as Warner is in "carefully developed meanings"
and as Wax is when he speaks of secondary socialization. But he
stops short of recognizing that these can be made external descriptive lists and used in a more objective fashion. This is Warner's
point when he says that these meanings are "part of our evidence."

My central criticism of *Verstehen,* however, is not this failure
to recognize the externalizability of the catalog; the major error
committed by Weber, by Munch, and by other supporters of
Verstehen (as well as its critics) is the failure to distinguish this
part of the procedure from the *inference* that the meanings lie in
the minds of the actors.

Many proponents of *Verstehen* and related methods imply or
even claim that the method involves some special form of communication which allows the scientist more direct access than normal
to what is in the mind of the other. This involves a naive view of
communication in which it is conceived that something is *conveyed*
from one mind to another. Thus, Munch (1957:31) says that the
physical characteristics ("form") of the act

> ... serves, within the framework of a cultural situation, as a
> symbol by which the specific meaning of a particular action
> is conveyed from actor to respondent as well as ... to the
> observer provided he knows the 'language.'

The basic fact of communication is that it occurs only as two
or more people jointly make the inference that what each finds in
his catalog is what the other is finding in his and thus what the symbol "means to me" by my act of catalog reference is what it means
to him by his act of reference. This inference is made viable not
only because we can observe the action implications of the inference, but because we can then turn our language into a metalan-
guage to talk about the inference. That is, we *confirm* the inference by other experience. Communication (as opposed to mere
message transmittal) occurs only when these three steps are
present: the act of reference by each participant, the act of inference by each, and the acts of confirmation. This avenue is

also open to the researcher if his problem requires this kind of data, but it is a step that is unnecessary for the observation of action and must be distinguished from it.

The observation of action as I have defined it here does not imply that the concept of the structured act nor the meanings identified are what the actors *now* have in their minds. We may wish to make this inference, but this is a separate operation from observation and has nothing to do with the objectivity of the observational procedure. It may be a valid inference and it may be proper to assume that actors continue to perform the structured acts that we see only so long as the conception of the act is "in their minds," but this is a separate problem from that of the observation of action in terms of social units.

In summary, then, social acts are complex patterns in terms of which participants structure their activity. These unit acts are conventional and are in most cases named. Their observation requires the development by the observer of a set of descriptions of these acts against which he compares the observed activity and in terms of which he records his observations. Social acts are thus different units of action than behavior which is the observation of activity with quite a different set of descriptions.

The essential character of the procedure is that the observer make the judgment that what he sees does or does not agree with a previously developed description of acts or catalog of meanings. Whether the degree of reliability required necessitates the externalization of the list or permits it to remain as part of the professional skill of the observer depends upon the requirements of the research problem.

This is neither a new conception nor a new method. Competent field workers in sociology and anthropology have been using this procedure for many years. I have attempted merely to formalize the conception and to make the method explicit in the hope that we can reduce some of the irrelevant arguments over the objectivity of the sociological enterprise. Furthermore, the recognition of the essential criteria of the method and especially the separation of the *verstehen* inference from the observation of meaning should have some extended implications for our theories of action and of meaning.

NOTES

1.   Bolton (1963), for example, says that the behaviorist view claims that it alone has a legitimate claim to scientific status and correctly notes that this is contrary to the trend toward multiple perspectives which makes possible objective orientations toward social process.

2.   An excellent example is presented in an unsigned article that appeared in the "Field Notes and Methods" column of *Applied Anthropology* a number of years ago. The author, driven by the need to have certified objectively, proposed that in order to study a ritual dance in a primitive society we should not do what anthropologists have always done, that is, carefully inquire of the participants as to the acts and their meanings. Rather said he, we should project upon the stage a three-dimensional grid and with a stopwatch, plot the physical movements in space and time. It is obvious that this procedure would give us no data by which to distinguish the random and irrelevant from the organized, meaningful, and pertinent.

REFERENCES

Becker, H. S., and B. Geer, 1957, "Participant observation and interviewing." *Human Organization* 16 (Fall): 28–32.

Bolton, C. D., 1963, "Is sociology a behavioral science?" *Pacific Sociology Review* VI (Spring): 3–9.

Chafe, W. L., 1965, "Meaning in language." *Formal Semantic Analysis,* special issue of *American Anthropologist* 67 (October): 23.

Hanson, Norwood R., 1965, *Patterns of Discovery*. Cambridge, England: Cambridge University Press.

Melville, Herman, 1923, *Typee*. New York: Dodd, Mead and Co.

Munch, P. A., 1957, "Empirical science and Max Weber's *Verstehende Soziologie.*" *American Sociological Review* 22 (February): 29.

Schneider, D. M., 1965, "American kin terms and terms for kinsmen: a critique of Goodenough's componential analysis of Yankee kinship terminology." *Formal Semantic Analysis,* special issue of *American Anthropologist* 67 (October): 289.

Warner, W. Lloyd, 1959, *The Living and the Dead.* New Haven: Yale University Press.

Wax, M. L., 1967, "On misunderstanding *verstehen*: a reply to Abel." *Sociology and Social Research* 51 (April): 323–333.

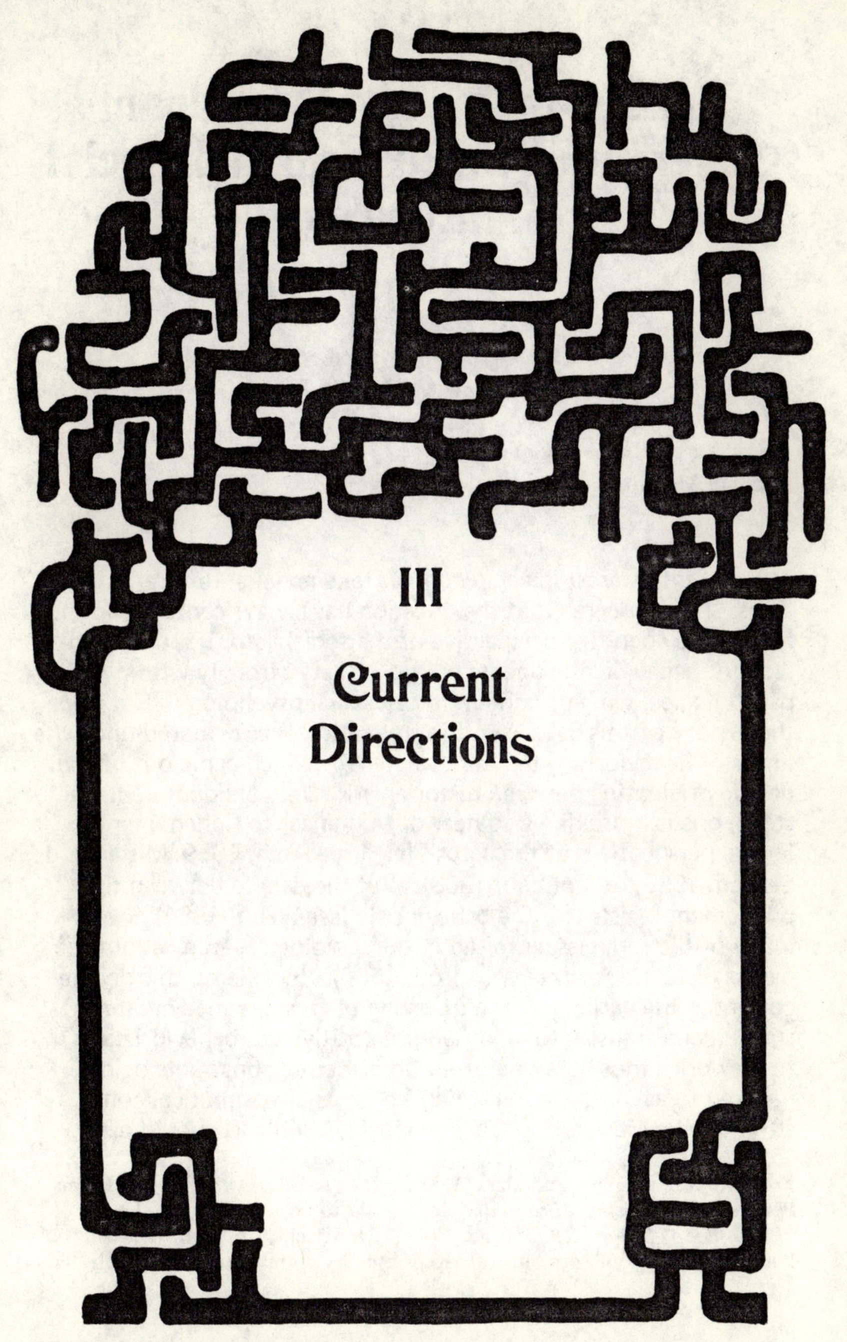
III

Current
Directions

8

Understanding and Participant Observation in Cultural and Social Anthropology

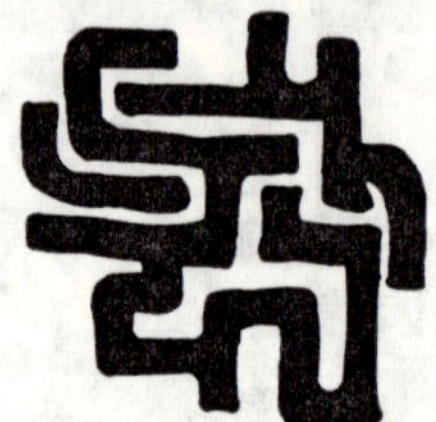

Michael Martin

The current interest in *verstehen* has taken several different directions. To the degree that the question has always centered upon role of the cognitive perspective of the social actor upon his subsequent behavior, the debate continues very strongly within the psychological wing of contemporary social psychology. But since the history of this debate within psychology has centered upon the limits of behaviorism, the term *verstehen* (which came out of the debate originating between historians) is rarely encountered. Instead, one is more likely to hear of references to "phenomenological perspectives of the actor" (e.g., see Asch, 1959; Misiak and Sexton, 1966; or McLeod, 1968). Yet the debate between the phenomenologists and the behaviorists (see Wann, 1964) covers many of the same issues raised in the sociological arena about the merits of *verstehen* (see Winthrop, 1964). In general, this debate continues the earlier pattern of trying to fit subjective mental states (cognitions) into an otherwise positivistic (behavioristic) framework; thus here one often finds mental constructs being referred to as "intervening variables" or as "hypothetical constructs" (see MacCorquodale and Meehl, 1948). It should also

From Robert S. Cohen and Marx W. Wartofsky (eds.), *Boston Studies in the Philosophy of Science: Proceedings of the Boston Colloquium for the Philosophy of Science 1966/1968*, Vol. 4. Dordrecht, Holland: D. Reidel Publishing Co., 1968, pp. 303–30. Reprinted by permission of the publisher.

be mentioned that within the psychological arena, largely outside the *verstehen* debate but very relevant to it, there has been a continuing concern with the empirical problems surrounding interpersonal perception (see Tagiuri, 1969). Since this literature deals with men's abilities to correctly perceive the motives and intentions of other men, and with the errors and problems therein, its implications and generalizations must include the social scientist's limitations and difficulties in making such inferences. If men in daily interaction with one another cannot understand one another fully, how fully can we expect such understanding on the part of man making inferences from the historical record?

Although the current debates within psychology between the behaviorists and phenomenologists are relevant to the *verstehen* debate, the issue in its original terms has become focused within modern sociology, especially in its wing of social psychology (once— possibly more properly—called psychological sociology). Within sociology the general trend toward bringing *verstehen* into the naturalistic perspective, primarily through the symbolic interactionist tradition initiated by G. H. Mead, has continued. But this concern with legitimizing *verstehen* has not taken the direction of trying to experimentally establish its validity (although some work has attempted to show the interrelations between attitudes and behavior). The effort has been to take it out of the hands of the armchair theorist and place it as a working device into the hands of those involved with the cultural meaning-structures through participant observation. This form of "naturalism" (see Lofland, 1967) in field studies has largely been a means of trying to empirically deal with the *verstehen* problem (see Schwartz and Merten, 1971).

In the following essay philosopher Michael Martin examines some of the problems in obtaining *verstehen* through participant understanding.

—MT

There was a time when cultural and social anthropologists did not do participant observation. Sir James Frazer, famous anthropologist of yesteryear, was once asked if he ever lived amongst savages. It is reported that he held up his hands "as though to ward off even the thought" and answered "God forbid!"[1]

Today things are quite different; field work and in particular participant observation seems, as one critic has put it, an initiation rite into the cult of professional anthropology.[2] How accurate this anthropological characterization of anthropology is I do not know. But it does seem to be true that great stress is laid on the method of participant observation in the profession today.

We will not consider here the anthropological significance of this phenomenon; after all this is a job for anthropologists or sociologists and not for philosophers. The philosophical questions connected with participant observation are rather different. First we want to know what "participant observation" means. As we shall see the term is not clear and several things have been meant by it. Secondly, we want to know whether there is any methodological justification for participant observation in any of its various senses in cultural and social anthropology. After all there may be good methodological reasons why anthropologists have stressed participant observation and good reasons for its having the significance it does seem to have within the profession. In particular, we shall try to determine the relevance of participant observation in the various senses analyzed for understanding a community. This is necessary because the method of participant observation seems to be closely connected in anthropological thought with the goal of understanding a community. Indeed, so important is the notion of understanding for the evaluation of participant observation that it will be necessary to analyze it before we begin on participant observation.

The paper will thus be divided into three parts. In the first part we will consider the meaning of "scientific understanding" in anthropology taking some time to separate out other concepts that may be confused with such understanding. In the second part of the paper we will consider the meaning of "participant observation" in anthropology, clarifying and separating different senses to be found in anthropological literature. In the third part of the paper we will consider the methodological relevance of participant observation for a scientific understanding of a community.

I. UNDERSTANDING A COMMUNITY

A. Scientific Understanding

Traditionally one of the major tasks of cultural and social anthropology has been to understand particular communities. In this respect, it has been suggested, anthropology is like history.[3] Cultural and social anthropology and history, it is said, are ideographic not nomothetic sciences; they do not aim at discovering laws or theories but in understanding particular phenomena.

Now whether such a description of cultural anthropology is accurate we need not decide here. Nor need we enter into two other closely related controversies: the question of whether anthropologists, although they may not aim to discover laws, nevertheless use laws in understanding particular communities; the question of whether anthropologists should aim to discover laws even if they do not do so.

Whatever the answers to these two questions and whatever the accuracy of the description of anthropology as an ideographic science, it does seem to be true that anthropologists have often aimed at understanding some particular community.

What does *understanding* a community mean? Although the term 'understanding' may be used in many senses in science and ordinary life, there is one sense that stands out. This might be called scientific or factual understanding. In this sense to understand something – a person, a subject, a community, and so on – is to know certain facts about the person, theory or community.[4] Thus in the case of persons, expressions like, 'Jones understands Smith' are often reducible to expressions of the form 'Jones knows that P_1 and P_2 and ... P_n, where $P_1, P_2 ..., P_n$ refer to certain facts about Smith. What sort of facts these are will usually be clear from the context. Sometimes the facts concern Smith's motivation, his purposes or his character; at other times the facts will be facts of his social or cultural background and their relation to his present behavior. I interpret the term 'fact' quite broadly here. One fact about Smith that Jones might have to know in some context to understand Smith is that Smith's behavior is subsumable under certain laws. The present analysis remains neutral with respect to the question of whether knowledge of such facts would be necessary.[5] In any case, conceived in this way, understanding a person seems to be reducible to knowing certain facts about him. We call this type of knowledge propositional knowledge.[6] Propositional knowledge is simply knowledge that something is the case. In the case of Jones and Smith, Jones' understanding Smith consists in Jones' having certain propositional knowledge of Smith, i.e., knowledge that certain things are true about Smith.

Where the object of understanding is not a person a similar kind of analysis seems possible. To say that Jones understands psychoanalysis or Newton's Theory is usually to say that Jones has some particular kind of propositional knowledge. Again the context usually makes clear what this propositional knowledge will be. The suggestion is often that Jones' propositional knowledge consists in knowing that phychoanalysis or Newton's Theory has certain important structural properties or that the parts of these theories fit together in a certain way; at other times the suggestion is that the propositional knowledge consists in knowing certain facts about the history of psychoanalysis or physics.

The same sort of thing could be said about understanding a community. Understanding a community seems to consist in having certain propositional knowledge about this community. Again what this knowledge will be will depend on the context of the inquiry. Sometimes understanding a community may consist in knowing that certain aspects of the community are related to one another in certain ways. Thus to say that John Beattie understands Bunyoro[7] may mean only that Beattie knows that certain social institutions in Bunyoro are related to each other in certain ways, forming what has been called a functional system. In other contexts understanding a community may consist in knowing that the community has such and such a historical development.

It should be clear that the present analysis is opposed to the view that there is only one set of facts which, if known, gives understanding of a community. In anthropology, understanding a community will be relative to the perspective taken by the anthropologist, the theory utilized in the investigation, and the purposes of the investigation. A community can be understood functionally, historically, and in other ways,[8] although given certain purposes some ways may be better than others. However all these different ways of understanding on the present analysis come down to having propositional knowledge about the community.

B. Being Understanding

Another notion of understanding which may not be clearly separated in anthropological thought from factual or scientific understanding is that of being understanding toward a community. [9] Now being understanding toward something or someone involves manifesting a certain attitude; one is understanding toward a person or group, for instance, if one is sympathetic, patient and tolerant towards the person or group.

It may be true that nowadays part of the ethical creed of the anthropological profession is humanitarianism and that part of this humanitarian attitude may be a sympathetic and tolerant attitude toward the community studied; that anthropologists are expected to be understanding toward the people they study. It must be stressed that however strong this commitment may be among field anthropologists and however justified it is on ethical grounds, there is no logical connection between this ethical posture and factual understanding of a community. As far as the logic of the two concepts is concerned, an anthropologist could fail to be understanding toward a community he studies and yet from a scientific standpoint understand the community very well; moreover, he might be understanding toward the community he studies yet have little scientific understanding of the community. To be sure, although there is no logical connection between these two concepts there might be some close practical connection. This might be true for a number of reasons: a failure to be understanding toward a community might be manifested in the anthropologist's behavior; this behavior might cause offense; as a result, the anthropologist might be denied access to vital information; this denial of vital information would in turn prevent scientific understanding of the community.

I say 'might' because the degree of intolerance a community can tolerate from a visiting anthropologist without closing down necessary sources of information is not completely known. It may well vary from community to community and from anthropologist to anthropologist. We may suspect at least that in some communities a high degree of intolerance and lack of sympathy can be expressed by the anthropologist and yet a high degree of scientific understanding of that community still be achieved. Malinowski's recent diary,[10] for example, indicates that Malinowski often felt and expressed great hatred toward the Trobriand Islanders; he was often not understanding toward them. Yet his study of these people[11] is usually considered to be a landmark in ethnographic understanding, i.e., he is considered to have scientific understanding of the community.

C. Empathy and Understanding

A discussion of understanding in anthropology is surely not complete without some mention of the notion of empathy. It is important to discuss the notion since empathy is often confused with the two notions of understanding I have already analyzed.

1. The Adoption Sense. I take it that on one common view, to say that someone empathizes with a person or group is to say that he 'puts himself' in the other's place, i.e., he adopts the attitudes, views, emotions, thought patterns, and so on of a person or group; he sees the world and emotionally reacts to the world in the same way as the person or group sees it and reacts to it. Thus an empathizing visiting anthropologist would see and think what the natives saw and thought, he would feel what the natives felt, and so on. Let us call this sense of 'empathy' the *adoption* sense of empathy. It might be said that only by this sort of empathy can the anthropologist understand the community at issue.

To evaluate this position one must sharply distinguish it from another position that may easily be confused with it. It has been maintained by some students of anthropological methodology that it is only by knowing that the natives have the beliefs, goals and attitudes they do have that one understands them. But it is one thing to say this and an entirely different thing to insist that it is only by seeing, feeling, and believing what the natives see, feel, and believe that understanding can be achieved. In short, there is a vast difference between *having* knowledge that people have such and such beliefs, goals and attitudes and *adopting* such beliefs, goals and attitudes. To make this point clear consider the following two expressions:

1. Beattie knows that the Nyoro have a suspicious attitude towards Europeans.

2. Beattie adopted the same suspicious attitude toward Europeans that the Nyoro have.

Notice that only in the second expression is there any question of empathy in the adoption sense. Notice also that these two expressions are logically independent. Beattie might know that Nyoro have a certain attitude without adopting that attitude. Beattie might, for instance, be psychologically incapable of being suspicious of Europeans although he knew perfectly well that the Nyoro are suspicious. Moreover, Beattie might adopt this attitude without knowing that the Nyoro have this attitude. For instance he might lack sufficient evidence that the Nyoro are suspicious. This would preclude his knowing that they do have such an attitude on most analyses of propositional knowledge. But it would not prevent him from adopting this attitude.

This example illustrates that propositional knowledge of people's beliefs, goals and attitudes is possible without empathy with the people in the adoption sense. And it is clear that this is true in general: scientific understanding as we have analyzed it in terms of propositional knowledge is possible without empathy in the adoption sense.

Indeed, empathy in this sense is at times incompatible with scientific understanding. For to empathize with a community in this sense may involve adopting their beliefs about their own culture and themselves. However, these beliefs may well be false and distorted and thus preclude scientific understanding. For example, suppose an anthropologist empathized with the natives of some community. This empathizing, let us suppose, involves adopting one of their false beliefs. For example suppose John Beattie in empathizing with the Nyoro believed that not p where not p is some false proposition about Bunyoro. On one standard analysis of propositional knowledge Beattie could not know that p if he believed that not p. If his knowing that p was essential to his understanding Bunyoro, his empathizing would have precluded his understanding Bunyoro.

Furthermore, empathizing with a community may at times be incompatible with being understanding toward the community. Recall that to be understanding toward a community is to be sympathetic and tolerant toward the community. But it is possible that an anthropologist could not in certain communities at one and the same time be both sympathetic and empathetic in the adoption sense. For to empathize with the natives in the present sense is at least to adopt the attitudes of the natives. But one attitude found in certain communities may be an attitude of intolerance and lack of sympathy toward everyone. Surely one could not at the same time be both sympathetic toward the natives and unsympathetic toward everyone.

I conclude that empathy in the adoption sense is usually irrelevant to the scientific understanding of a community and that under certain conditions it is incompatible with it. I conclude also that empathy in the adoption sense is at times incompatible with being understanding toward a community.

2. *The Assimilation Sense.* There is another sense of 'empathy' that must be distinguished from the adoption sense. This sense is suggested by a statement by Nadel. He remarked: "Much in this process of 'empathy' can be reduced to simple empirical facts. Complete knowledge and ready use of the vernacular; long sojourn in the community; and above all, the cumulative effect of constant enquiries into everything that is observed – all these built up a familiarity with the native society which in more poetic language, one might call 'entering into the soul of the savage.' When you find yourself making jokes at which the people laugh (no mean achievement, this); when you have mastered their ways of linking concepts and adducing proof, or when you can predict with fair accuracy what X will do and feel in such and such a situation, you have accomplished an adequate 'assimilation'."[12]

I take it that in this passage Nadel is using 'empathy' in a sense other than the adoption sense. In this new sense to say that someone has empathy with a group is to say that the person can get around in the group easily, that he speaks their language, is on joking terms with them, and so on. In this sense of 'empathy' empathy seems to consist in the utilization of a complex skill. To use Ryle's notion, empathy in this sense is the utilization of a type of knowledge how, or, as it has recently been called, procedural knowledge.[13] Borrowing from Nadel, one might call this sense of empathy the *assimilation* sense.

These two senses of 'empathy' distinguished here are logically independent. One might move about smoothly in a group, be on joking terms with them, and so on without adopting the beliefs, goals, and attitudes of the members of the group although it might be necessary at times to act as if one had adopted some of these beliefs and goals and attitudes. One might also adopt a people's beliefs, goals, and attitudes and yet not move smoothly in the group. For instance the group might not believe that one had adopted their beliefs, goals, and attitudes. This belief might prevent assimilation.

As we shall see in a moment the assimilation sense of 'empathy' is closely connected with one sense of 'participant observation.' Because of this close connection, the relevance of the assimilation sense of 'empathy' to scientific understanding will be discussed later when we discuss the relevance of participant observation for scientific understanding.

There is no logical connection between the assimilation sense of 'empathy' and being understanding toward a community. One could have empathy with a community in the assimilation sense and yet not be understanding toward the community – although one might have to act *as if* one were understanding toward it in order to be assimilated. Indeed, the process of becoming assimilated in a community may in certain cases breed contempt rather than sympathy. (Malinowski's experience is perhaps an example of this.)

Conversely one can be understanding toward a community without being assimilated in the community. Indeed, being understanding toward a community is possible over great periods of time and spans of space. Thus some contemporary classicists are understanding toward classical Greek civilization although these men could hardly be said to be assimilated in ancient Greek society.

To be sure, under certain conditions assimilation in a community may be conducive to being understanding toward a community; and conversely, under other circumstances not being assimilated in a community may prevent understanding toward the community from developing. However, under what conditions this may happen is unclear and is a matter for empirical investigation.

II. THE MEANING OF PARTICIPANT OBSERVATION

Although the term 'participant observation' is widely used in social science literature, little attempt has been made to separate the different strands involved and to clarify issues. There have been, however, some attempts to specify different senses of the term. In a well known article Becker and Geer differentiate different senses of 'participant observation' and we will consider some of these here.[14]

A. Participant Observation as Being a Member of a Group

1. The Native Sense. In one of Becker and Geer's senses to say that someone is a participant observer of a community is to say that one is a member of the community. This definition is hardly helpful until we are clearer on what being a member of a community involves. For example, is John Beattie a member of the African community of Bunyoro if he lives in this community or are only the Nyoro members of Bunyoro. To clarify this situation let us differentiate between two senses of being a member of a community: the sense in which the Nyoro are members of Bunyoro, let us call this the 'native sense' of being a member of a community; the sense in which Beattie was a member, let us call it the "living-in" sense of being a member of a community.

It should be noted that although most of the Nyoro are members of the Bunyoro community in the living-in sense, not all are; presumably some of the Nyoro are away and are not actually living in the community at some particular time. Thus in the living-in sense Beattie was a participant observer of Bunyoro in 1951 although some of the Nyoro were not participant observers in 1959 in this sense. Moreover, all the Nyoro are participant observers in the native sense of participant observer of Bunyoro by virtue of *their* cultural background although Beattie could never be a participant observer in this sense by virtue of *his* cultural background. It seems apparent that anthropologists are not interested in the native sense of participant observation; it is the living-in sense that has relevance for them.

2. The Living-In Sense. But what does living in a community involve in anthropological field work? Does it involve living in a

community as the natives live? The answer is that it does but only
to a certain extent. The extent will depend on the anthropologist
and the culture. For Malinowski living in a community involved
isolating oneself from white men, taking residence in the village,
eating native food, seeking out native entertainment and conversation. Beattie did all of this and more: he gave banana beer
parties, and even did some native work. On the other hand, for
many anthropologists living in a community does not include
dressing in native garb, engaging in native sexual practices, giving
up certain Western customs. Thus it is not strictly speaking true,
as Frazer suggests, that Malinowski "lived as a native" in his study
of Trobriand Islanders.[15]

   Why anthropologists should adopt some of the practices of a
people and not others is an interesting question and we will consider it in a moment.

3. *The Assimilation Sense.* However, one needs to make a finer
distinction in 'the living-in' sense of participant observation in
order to do justice to anthropological method. For most anthropologists are not merely interested in living in a community in the
sense just specified. One might live in a community in this sense
and yet be unable to operate in the community with ease and com-
fort and familiarity: one might not know one's way about with
respect to the customs of the people. It was only after some time
that Malinowski said that he learned how to behave and to a certain extent acquired 'the feeling' for the natives. good and bad
manners.[16] To say that Malinowski was a participant observer
in a community is to say that he lived in a community and knew
his way about the community socially. In this sense to be a participant observer is to utilize a certain social know-how while living
among the natives.

   It should be noted that this sense of participant observation is
identical to the assimilation sense of empathy specified earlier.
Indeed, let us call this sense of being a member of a community the
assimilation sense of being a member of a community. Notice that
in this sense, the extent to which an anthropologist is a member of
a community and thus the extent to which he is a participant observer in this community will be a matter of degree.

It should also be noted that the extent to which an anthropologist follows native customs and practices may be closely connected with the degree of social know-how he develops and utilizes in the culture. A following of native customs and practices to a certain degree seems essential for developing social know-how. On the other hand the following of particular native customs and practices may bring ridicule and hostility and actually prevent social know-how from developing. The extent to which the customs and practices must be followed in order to achieve the maximal social know-how will undoubtedly vary from culture to culture and anthropologist to anthropologist. In any case, the possibility of adverse effects of following some customs of the natives does provide some methodological grounds for not going completely native.

Notice, however, that although it might be necessary for an anthropologist to follow some of the customs of the natives in order to gain social know-how and to avoid adopting others in order to maintain this know-how, it would not be necessary that the anthropologist adopt any of the natives' *beliefs, goals,* or *attitudes.* To be sure, it might be necessary for the anthropologist to act *as if* he had adopted some of them. But this is a different matter. Thus having empathy with the natives in the adoption sense of 'empathy' specified earlier, is not a necessary condition for participant observation in the assimilation or living-in senses just specified.

Of course, some methodologists have defined 'participant observation' in such a way that it includes being empathetic in the adoption sense. [17] On the other hand, others have suggested that the expression 'participant' excludes empathy in the adoption sense. [18] It seems to me that this latter view comes closer to the truth. As we shall see in a moment some of the standard senses of 'participant observation' in social science literature would tend in some cases to exclude empathy in the adoption sense.

Taking our point of departure from Becker and Geer we have thus far characterized two senses of 'participant observation' that seem quite relevant for anthropology and yet do not involve empathy in the adoption sense. First the living-in sense: in this sense a participant observer is a person who lives in a culture and adopts some of the customs and practices of the people. Second, the assimilation sense: in this sense a participant observer is a person who lives in a community, develops some social know-how, and is assimilated to a certain extent in the community. We have emphasized that these two senses are closely related to one another. To gain social know-how in a culture involves living in the community and following certain customs and practices of the natives. However gaining social know-how may also involve not following other customs and practices.

So far we have simply tried to clarify and expand one of Becker and Geer's condensed characterizations of participant observation. However, even with this clarification and expansion there is a fundamental omission in Becker and Geer's account. It leaves out all mention of the fact that the person living in the culture and having certain social know-how has as one of his purposes observing the culture. A person who lived in the culture and had certain social know-how of the culture would normally not be considered to be a participant observer unless he had as one of his purposes observing the culture, i.e., studying it. Missionaries and traders would not normally be considered participant observers of a culture even if they lived in the culture and gained a certain social know-how unless they were attempting to study the culture as well as save souls or sell merchandise.

Thus the living-in sense of participant observation must be amended as follows: A participant observer is a person who lives in a culture, adopting some of the customs and practices of the natives, and has as one of his purposes while living in the culture observing the culture. The definition of 'participant observation' in the assimilation sense would have to be modified along similar lines.

Once it is admitted that this qualification is needed, empathy in the adoption sense would in certain cases be ruled out. To empathize with a person or group in the adoption sense is to adopt all the goals, attitudes and beliefs of the person or group. Moreover, since the basic idea is to put oneself in the other person's place, it would presumably involve repressing or eliminating some of one's own goals, attitudes and beliefs; namely those goals, attitudes and beliefs that are different from those of the person or group being empathized with. But then if a participant observer is a person who by definition has as his purpose the observation of the members of the group and the members of the group do not have this as one of their goals, being a participant observer of a group and

being a complete empathizer with the group in the adoption sense
at one and the same time is ruled out. This, of course, does not
rule out being a participant observer in these senses at certain times
and empathizing with a group at different times. Nor does it rule
out adopting some of a group's goals, attitudes, and beliefs, i.e.,
partially empathizing, and being a participant observer in these
senses at the same time. But it does seem to rule out *complete* empathy and participant observation in these senses at the same time,
in certain cases.

B. Participant Observation as Posing as a Member of a Community

Becker and Geer differentiate another sense of participant observation. In this sense to say that someone is a participant observer
is to say that the person is posing as a member of a group or community. To achieve participant observation in this sense would be
difficult, if not impossible, in many typical field situations. Consider the native sense of being a member of a community. The anthropologist as a participant observer would have to pose as a member of the community under investigation. Beattie in this sense of
participant observation would have to pose as a Nyoro, a most un-
likely prospect! As Herskovits has noted, the white anthropologist
in a black man's culture has a "high degree of social visibility";[19]
it is rather difficult to think of Beattie or Malinowski attempting to
pass themselves off as one of their black subjects by disguises,
make up, and so on.

Consider the living-in sense of being a member of a community. It is difficult to see how an anthropologist could pose as
someone living in a community to the community, when the community is small and isolated as is typical in anthropological studies.
For example, how could Beattie have convinced the members of
the small Bunyoro village he wished to study that he was himself
living in the village? It might have been possible for Beattie to pose
as someone living in a small Bunyoro community to his friends at
Oxford and even to members of another distant village but hardly
to the members of the small village he did study.

I think it can safely be said that participant observation in
this sense has such severe limitations in most anthropological
field work that it can be ignored, and we will so ignore it. In any

case, this sense also would have to be modified in terms of the purposes of the person posing as a member of the group: the person posing as a member of a group would have to have as one of his purposes the observation of the group to be a participant observer.

C. Participant Observation as the Role of an Observer in a Community

Becker and Geer distinguish another type of participant observer. In this sense to be a participant observer one joins a group as "one who is there to observe." Although this kind of participant observation is not completely clarified, what they seem to have in mind is roughly this: on certain occasions a social scientist joins a group and makes it known that he is there to study the group. He takes the role of an observer or student of the group. Let us call this sense of 'participant observation' the *observer-role* sense of participant observation. One gathers that it was this type of participant observation that Becker and Geer themselves used in their study.

But what does joining the group consist of in the observer-role sense? Does it consist in living in the group, being assimilated to a certain extent, gaining a certain social know-how? Does this sense include the living-in sense and assimilation sense of participant observation specified above? Sometimes it does. Beattie, for instance, came to his Bunyoro village as an observer. He announced to the assembled villagers at the beginning of his stay:

> "I have come to your country to learn your language, and about your history, your traditions and your customs and the way you live. I have come from a big school in Europe where grown-ups are taught, including some who come to Africa..." [20]

This speech and his subsequent behavior placed Beattie in the role of observer of the village while in the village. Nevertheless this did not prevent him from living in the village, gaining a certain amount of social know-how and to a certain extent being assimilated.

Although sometimes – as in Beattie's case – being a participant observer in an observer-role sense includes being a participant observer in the living-in and assimilation senses, there is no necessity in this. These senses of 'participant observation' are logically distinct. One could join a group in the role of an observer and yet never gain any social know-how, never be assimilated to any extent into the group, and adopt very few of the customs of the group.

Anthropologists who are participant observers in the living-in and assimilation senses of participant observation do not always take the role of an observer. Some argue that the fact that they are studying the community they are living in should be hidden from the natives. Florence Kluckhohn,[21] for example, stresses the necessity for the participant observer not to disclose that he is studying the group while living in the group. She argues that such a disclosure might distort the information received while living in the community and indeed prevent the anthropologist from obtaining information that he might otherwise have received. Kluckhohn, it should be noted, was in a fortunate position: for reasons we need not go into here she was able to live in a New Mexican village and study the people without any need for disclosing that she was studying them.

Whether Kluckhohn's approach would be possible or even desirable in all cases is uncertain. Could Beattie, for example, have been a participant observer in the assimilation sense in his Bunyoro village without having taken the role of an observer of the group? What pretext could he have used to start to live in the village? What would have happened if it had been discovered that he was lying? Moreover, is it really true that the observer-role he did take distorted his information as Kluckhohn seems to maintain? We do not know the answers to these questions. Much more information about human psychology and culture will have to be secured before they can be answered with any confidence.

One suspects, however, that Kluckhohn's view is much too simple. Whether or not observer-role participant observation will distort will depend on many factors including the type of information one is after and the culture under study. For instance, there might be certain types of information which could be gathered by observer-role participant observation with much more success than by other types of observation. Moreover, the very role of an observer may loosen tongues and provoke confessions in certain people under certain circumstances. A similar phenomenon has been noticed by some anthropologists: it has been noticed that in some cases anthropologists have access to certain information because they are non-natives. Thus far from their outsider role being a handicap, it may under certain conditions be a help.

III. THE JUSTIFICATION OF PARTICIPANT OBSERVATION

Now that we have discussed several different senses of 'participant observation' we will consider some possible methodological justifications for participant observation.

A. Participant Observation as a Sufficient Condition for Scientific Understanding of a Community

One possible methodological reason for the use of participant observation in anthropology could be that participant observation in a community is a sufficient condition for achieving scientific understanding of the community. It seems to me, however, that this thesis is mistaken no matter what sense of 'participant observation' one considers.

Consider the living-in sense of participant observation. Surely living in a community and following some of the customs and practices of the natives with the purpose of observing them does not guarantee scientific understanding of the community in the sense defined above. This is true for any number of reasons. For instance, while living in a community one may have to adopt the customs or practices of one particular social class and this may alienate one from another social class in the community, in turn preventing one from getting needed information. Under precisely what conditions such alienation and information blockage would occur is not completely clear at the present time. We do know that it sometimes happens. Beattie, for example, had the following choice in Bunyoro: if he lived with the King and his court, he would alienate the people; if he lived with the people, he would alienate the King and his court. Beattie chose the latter course of action and as a result much of the inner workings of the King and his court remained unknown to him. There seems to be no doubt that living with the people and adopting their customs actually prevented Beattie from gaining complete scientific understanding of a certain major social relation in Bunyoro.[22] It should be noted that this was indeed a loss for Beattie since because of his theoretical orientation he was committed to studying all the major social relations of the Bunyoro. The curious fact is that Beattie was also committed to doing participant observation in the living-in sense. The commitment to this method conflicted with full realization of his theoretical goal.

But even if there were no problem of alienation other problems remain. I have already mentioned that merely living in a community and adopting some of the customs of the natives will not necessarily bring about assimilation. Whether it will or not depends on many factors. And without this assimilation it may be impossible to get the sort of information one needs to understand the community.

Now consider the assimilation sense of 'participant observation.' At least one of the problems of the living-in sense remains. In becoming assimilated to one class of a community one may alienate another class; this in turn may block some important sources of information, in turn preventing scientific understanding.

There is another problem. Being assimilated in a community involves moving easily in the community, having a feeling for the manners and mores of the natives, and so on, but it does not in any way guarantee that scientific understanding of the community has been achieved. Scientific understanding of a community as we have specified it above consists in having certain propositional knowledge about the community. Being assimilated need not and often does not involve such propositional knowledge. One might be assimilated in a community and yet be ignorant of facts about the structure or history of the community which it would be necessary to know in order to understand the community given one's purposes and perspective.

Much the same sort of thing can be said for the observer-role sense of 'participant observation.' Announcing to the natives that one is there to observe them may be the kiss of death to one's research project. Even if one is allowed to stay after the disclosure, necessary information may be blocked by it. However, aside from these problems the mere fact of being in a certain role in a community, i.e., the role of an observer of that community, does not guarantee that any propositional knowledge has been obtained.

And since scientific understanding involves obtaining such knowledge, being in the role of an observer does not necessarily mean that scientific understanding has been achieved.

B. Participant Observation as a Necessary Condition for Scientific Understanding of a Community

It may be granted that participant observation in a community in the senses specified is not a sufficient condition for scientific understanding of the community. However, it may be maintained that participant observation is a necessary condition for scientific understanding. This certainly seems to be Beattie's view. He argues that "only by at least some participation in the community life" [23] can the anthropologist understand the community and that the "observer must live in and with the community he is studying; it is not enough to stay in a comfortable hotel or rest-home and to visit them for a few hours daily or less often."[24]

Before we can evaluate this contention it is necessary to clear up a certain ambiguity in the thesis. Is the claim that no person could scientifically understand a community unless the person himself was a participant observer in the community? Or is the claim rather that no person could scientifically understand a community unless some person or other was a participant observer in the community? Presumably it is the latter claim that is at issue since the former claim seems to have implications that are obviously false: no mere reader of anthropological literature could ever have scientific understanding of a community; an anthropologist who lived in a community could never communicate his scientific understanding of the community in his books and monographs. But surely this is mistaken. It may be true that anthropologists sometimes fail to give their readers any scientific understanding of a community. But they are hardly doomed to this failure; there seems to be no *a priori* reason to suppose they could not succeed.

The latter claim must be taken more seriously, however, but still we have a problem of clarification. What sense of 'participant observation' is at issue: the living-in sense, the assimilation sense, the observer-role sense? Let us interpret the thesis to be this: for all cultures someone's participant observation in one of the relevant senses is a necessary condition for understanding the culture. The thesis stated in this way has some difficulties.

It is worth pointing out initially that Beattie and most British social anthropologists investigate cultures that are still existing; and it is well known that British social anthropologists often have a definite ahistorical or even anti-historical orientation.[25] American cultural anthropologists, because of the types of cultures they have investigated, have been forced sometimes to use different methods than their British colleagues. Thus the alternative to participant observation is not always, as Beattie seems to suggest, traveling from a comfortable hotel or rest-home to "visit the natives a few hours daily or less." American anthropologists have sometimes wanted to investigate Indian civilizations that are virtually extinct. They have used old native informants and not participant observation[26] in their work; sometimes they have not even left their hotel. The informant has come to them.

Cornelius Osgood,[27] for example, reports his investigation of the old culture of the Northern Athapascans primarily by the use of the remarkable Indian informant Billy Williams. Williams, a man of remarkable intelligence and photographic recall, was interviewed by Osgood 8 hours a day for weeks on end. Williams on his own initiative would travel to remote settlements to quiz old Indian women and men on details he did not know and reported the results to Osgood. Williams would make models of the old buildings and of manufactured objects for Osgood in his spare time and would spend hours relating the intricate and complex old ceremonies and dances to Osgood. It is hard to accept the view that Osgood, because he was not a participant observer in the old culture, did not come to have a scientific understanding of old Northern Athapascan culture through the informant Williams.

Indeed, I am far from convinced that even in Beattie's own work participant observation in any of the senses at issue was necessary. Beattie's procedure was as follows: After studying all the written documents on the Bunyoro culture, Beattie went to Bunyoro and became a participant observer in the living-in, assimilation and observer-role senses in a small Bunyoro village; he learned the language, adopted some customs, observed the social relations, took notes and after 6 months returned to Oxford. In Oxford he studied his notes, continued to study the language, consulted with his teachers and after 4 months returned to Bunyoro. One gathers that on this visit he used very little participant observation. Primarily he used other methods: he used informants, studied court records and official documents, took surveys, gave questionnaires, had natives write essays, and so on.

One naturally wonders whether his first 6 months' visit as a participant observer in a small Bunyoro village was really necessary. Would it really have been impossible to proceed without this initial contact? Is there any particular piece of information that Beattie would not have obtained without the first 6 months of participant observation?

These questions must not be confused with another type of question. Was Beattie's stay in a Bunyoro village an enriching and aesthetically satisfying experience? Could this experience have been achieved in any other way? Could it have been achieved by non-participant observer methods? It is no doubt true that participant observation is often an enriching, moving and aesthetically significant experience for anthropologists. And it may also be true that such an experience is difficult or even impossible to achieve in other ways. But this, it seems to me, shows nothing about the necessity of participant observation for achieving scientific understanding. The question we are concerned with here is only: is there any good reason to suppose that every fact Beattie learned about Bunyoro's social structure – this was what Beattie was primarily interested in – could not have been learned from good informants and other non-participant observer methods? We are not interested in whether Beattie will always cherish his 6 months in a small Bunyoro village or whether this moving experience could not have been achieved in other ways.

It must be emphasized that Beattie advances very little in the way of explicit argument to substantiate his view that his 6 months as a participant observer was necessary for a scientific understanding of the Bunyoro. As far as I can discern, his belief that it was necessary rests upon two major consideration:

1. It is necessary to learn the native language of a culture to understand the culture. Unless he knew the language he would not have been able to check his informants and interpreters, compose questionnaires, gain insight into the natives' thinking. Six months alone as a participant observer where he was forced to use the language was an ideal way to achieve this linguistic knowledge.

2.   In his 6 months as a participant observer he got a certain feel for the culture. Without this initial exposure he would not have been able to ask his informants the right questions or compose an insightful questionnaire. Thus the first 6 months of participant observation could not have been eliminated.

These considerations, however, are hardly persuasive. Consider the first point.

Whether learning the native language is necessary for achieving understanding of a community we need not decide here, but it should be noted that not all anthropologists have believed that learning the language is essential in field work.[28] Let us grant, however, that learning the native language is essential. The most Beattie's argument shows is that the *best* way to learn the language would be through participant observation. It does not prove, however, that participant observation was a necessary condition for learning the native language and hence a necessary condition for achieving understanding. And it is surely mistaken to suppose that participant observation was a necessary condition for learning the native language in Beattie's case. Thus although Beattie did master the essentials of the native language while a participant observer presumably other methods were available to him, e.g., hiring a native tutor. Moreover, it is not completely obvious that participant observation is even the best way to learn a native language. So little is known about language learning that one might well take a skeptical attitude to this contention. For all we know at the present time a native tutor might well be a much better method.

In order to criticize Beattie's second point one need not belittle Beattie's idea of getting an initial feel of the culture. This initial and germinal exploratory period may indeed be necessary for all empirical research. The question is whether participant observation is necessary for gaining this feel. It should be recalled that anthropologists like Osgood who used a single informant like Billy Williams managed to get a feel for the old culture without participant observation. By asking the informant questions – perhaps stupid questions or perhaps by just letting the informant talk at random – one may get a feel for the culture. After a while more penetrating and intelligent questions can be asked.

It might be objected, however, that it was still necessary to have a participant observer in order to obtain any scientific understanding of, for example, the old North Athapascans' culture; that Billy Williams himself was the participant observer. But Williams was not presumably a participant observer in any of the senses at issue. Recall that to be a participant observer of a community in the senses under discussion one must have as one of one's purposes to observe or study the community at issue. Now although Billy Williams was a man of remarkable observing powers there is no good reason to suppose that he engaged in a purposeful study of the culture in which he lived while he lived there. It is true that Williams was a participant observer in the native-sense of participant observer. But as we have seen, this sense has little relevance to anthropological discussion of participant observation. Williams was an informant and the use of informants is *contrasted* with participant observation in the relevant senses in anthropological discussions.

Moreover, if we consider cultures that have long since perished, the dubiousness of the necessity of reports of participant observers even in the native-sense of participant observation, e.g., informants, becomes apparent. It does not seem to be true that one can have no scientific understanding of a culture without reports of natives. In reconstructions of prehistorical cultures archaeologists do not base their reconstructions on the reports of participant observers in any of the senses specified – even the native sense. Material artifacts such as coins, pottery, art work and so on of the old cultures may be the only source of evidence available. Thus Larco Hoyle[29] reconstructed the ancient Mochica culture of Peru primarily on the basis of scenes portrayed on grave pottery. Other investigators have reconstructed ancient cultures on similar evidence. [30]

It is important not to neglect the limitations of these kinds of reconstructions; on the other hand it is equally important not to belittle what they can achieve. And what they can achieve will depend on many factors. The type of material artifacts that are used, the kinds of cultural facts that are inferred, the strength of analogical reasoning that can be brought to bear, will all affect the understanding that these reconstructions can give.

It would be incorrect to say that these reconstructions always give us a great understanding of ancient cultures. But it is equally incorrect to say that they give us no understanding of these cultures. It seems correct to say that they do sometimes give us a moderate degree of understanding, although it may be easily admitted that different sorts of evidence could increase our understanding. The evidence obtained from informants and participant observation might well be evidence of this sort.

Since we have just made this small concession to the method of participant observation it is time to make another. There is a much weaker version of the thesis that participant observation is a necessary condition for understanding a culture. Instead of claiming that for *all* cultures someone's participant observation in one of the relevant senses is a necessary condition for anyone understanding the culture, the claim might rather be that for *some* cultures someone's participant observation in one of the relevant senses is a necessary condition for anyone understanding the culture, the claim might rather be that for *some* cultures someone's participant observation in one of the relevant senses is a necessary condition for anyone understanding the culture. This claim is not so obviously mistaken and indeed may even be true. It may be impossible at certain times in certain cultures to get reliable and trustworthy informants, direct non-participant observation may be impossible, no written history or literature may be available, archaeological reconstructions may be out of the question, and so on. Under these conditions participant observation may well have to be used if any understanding is to be achieved.

How often such conditions are realized is difficult to say. In any case, it remains to be shown that these conditions occur often enough to justify the great stress placed on participant observation by the anthropological profession.

C. Participant Observation as the Most Efficient Way of Obtaining Information of Certain Kinds

If we reject the view that participant observation is always a necessary condition for obtaining scientific understanding of a community, we may attempt to justify the widespread use of participant observation on other grounds. One might argue that participant observation is the most efficient way of obtaining certain kinds of information in a community and that these kinds of information are necessary for a scientific understanding. This tack is taken by Morris Zelditch. [31]

Zelditch argues that there are three types of information that social scientists in community studies are interested in obtaining: information about frequency distributions, e.g. the number of married women in the community; information about certain incidents in the community, e.g. a recent wedding in the community; information about rules or norms in the community, e.g. marriage rules. Moreover, there are three methods that social scientists use to obtain these three types of information: surveys, participant observation, informants.

Zelditch maintains that these three methods should be judged by two criteria: (a) informational adequacy, and (b) efficiency. Judged in these terms he finds the following: Survey method has the greatest informational adequacy and most efficiency with respect to frequency distributions; participant observation has the least. On the other hand, participant observation has the greatest information adequacy and most efficiency with respect to incidents; survey methods has the least. Use of informants has the most informational adequacy and most efficiency with respect to rules and norms; participant observation, although it has good informational adequacy, if inefficient in obtaining this kind of information.

Zelditch's contention, if correct, would indeed provide some justification for the widespread use of participant observation in anthropology. There are, however, certain questions one can raise about Zelditch's views.

First of all, it is unclear what Zelditch means by 'participant observation.' What sense of 'participant observation' is being used in his claim that participant observation is the best method to obtain information about certain incidents in a community? Certainly this will make a difference, since, as we have seen, certain types of participant observation may have particular problems in certain communities. For example, the role-observer type of participant observation may be difficult to carry out in certain types of communities and may be performed only at a great price.

Moreover, what is the range of his claims? Is Zelditch suggesting that participant observation in some sense is *always* more efficient and more informationally adequate in obtaining information about incidents in the community? What sort of incidents are these? If the incident occurred 40 years ago, far from participant observation in some sense being the best method, it is not possible to use it at all. An old reliable informant like Billy Williams may be an anthropologist's only hope. But this may be true even with a contemporary incident. For instance, if Beattie had suddenly discovered that an important and rare ceremony was to occur in a Bunyoro village close to the Bunyoro village he was a participant observer in, it would have been impossible for him to have obtained information about this incident by his participant observation. He was not a participant observer in the neighboring village and in several relevant senses of 'participant observer' it would have been impossible under normal circumstances to have become one in the needed time. If Beattie needed this information to obtain an understanding on Bunyoro culture, some nonparticipant observer method would have been his only hope.

Of course Beattie might have hoped that this rare ceremony would occur in the village in which he was a participant observer given enough time. However, he only had a limited time to perform his research and in any case a long wait would be inefficient.

Moreover, there may be certain kinds of contemporary incidents occurring in a community in which an anthropologist is a participant observer which are not and cannot be observed by the anthropologist. For instance, there may be secret ceremonies to which the anthropologist has no access despite his having lived in the community for an extended period of time and despite his having developed a sense of social know-how. In this case also it would be necessary to use trusted informants if any are available. To be sure, the anthropologist may maintain that given more time and patience these ceremonies will be opened to him. But the time and energy needed to gain entrance into the inner circle may well make other methods more efficient.

Of course, it may be admitted that in certain cultures under certain conditions relative to certain types of information participant observation in some of the senses discussed may be more efficient than other methods. But this is an extremely weak claim; indeed, it would hardly by itself justify any widespread use of participant observation or justify the status participant observation seems to enjoy in the profession.

CONCLUSION

The main conclusions of this paper are as follows:

1. Scientific understanding of a community consists in knowing certain facts about the community. What these facts are will depend on the context of inquiry.

2. Scientific understanding of a community is logically independent of being understanding toward a community although there may be certain important practical connections between achieving scientific understanding of a community and being understanding toward that community.

3. Being empathetic with a community in one important sense of the term (the adoption sense) is usually independent of both scientific understanding of the community and being understanding toward the community. Moreover, there are cases in which being empathetic is incompatible with understanding in both senses of understanding.

4. Participant observation in the senses specified here is neither a sufficient condition nor a necessary condition for achieving scientific understanding of all communities.

5. Moreover, participant observation is not in all cases the most efficient way of obtaining certain types of information.

6. However, it may be true that in certain cases participant observation is a necessary condition for achieving scientific understanding of a community and in certain cases it may be the most efficient way of obtaining needed information. How far ranging these cases are is uncertain. If anthropologists put great stress on participant observation as has been often claimed and if the number of such cases is small, this emphasis can not be justified on the methodological grounds here considered.[32]

Several cautions or perhaps disclaimers should be added to these conclusions:

1. It may be a myth that anthropologists do put great emphasis on participant observation as a method. If so, I am attacking a straw man, and I should get myself new 'native' informants since

I have gathered my impressions about the status of participant observation from people in or close to the profession.

2. Other methodological justifications might indeed be possible. Naturally, I have not exhausted all possible ones in my paper.

3. Even if no methodological justification is possible it does not follow that participant observation should be deemphasized in the profession for some other sort of justification may be possible. Participant observation may give anthropologists great enjoyment, pleasure, adventure and a sense of esprit de corps, for example, and this perhaps is all the justification that a widespread use of participant observation may need in anthropology.

One final thought: I have evaluated the relevance of participant observation for achieving scientific understanding, but it may be a mistake to suppose that anthropologists are after this type of understanding alone when they investigate some particular society or culture. Kroeber has noted that there is an aesthetic dimension to anthropological thought and method.[33] There is a sense of 'understanding' distinct from scientific understanding that I have not yet mentioned. For example, when one speaks of understanding a poem or painting or a piece of music one may well have something different in mind than knowing certain facts about the work of art.[34] Thus aesthetic understanding may indeed be analogous to what the anthropologist is after in understanding a culture or society and participant observation may be much more relevant to achieving this sort of understanding than to achieving scientific understanding. But a consideration of this suggestion is another paper.

NOTES

1. Patrick Gallagher's review of Malinowski's *A Diary in the Strict Sense of the Term*, in *New Republic*, June 17, 1967, p. 14.

2. I. C. Jarvie, *The Revolution In Anthropology*, The Humanities Press, New York, 1964, p. 29.

3. See, for example, E. E. Evans-Pritchard's 'Social Anthropology: Past and Present,' *Man* 50 (1950), 118–124; Conrad M. Arensberg, 'Anthropology as History,' in K. Polanyi *et al.*, *Trade and Market in Early Empires.*

4. It is important to note here we are discussing the notion of understanding something, i.e. expressions of the form x understands y. In these expressions 'understands' takes a noun or noun phrase as its grammatical object. We are not discussing here expressions where 'understands' takes some propositional clause as its grammatical object. For an analysis of these latter kinds of expressions see May Brodbeck, 'Meaning and Action,' in *Readings in the Philosophy of Social Science* (ed. by May Brodbeck), Macmillan Co., New York, 1968.

5. Cf. C. G. Hempel, *Aspects of Scientific Explanation,* The Free Press, New York 1965, p. 488. According to Hempel to understand a phenomena is to show that it fits "into a nomic nexus." In our terms this would involve knowing that the phenomena fits into a nomic nexus. According to the present analysis Hempel's view would be a special case of scientific understanding.

6. For a discussion of propositional knowledge see Israel Scheffler, *Conditions of Knowledge,* Scott, Foresman, Chicago, 1965.

7. See John Beattie, *Understanding an African Community: Bunyoro*, Holt, Rinehart and Winston, New York, 1965.

8. Cf. Leslie White, 'History, Evolutionism and Functionalism: Three Types of Interpretation of Culture,' *SJA*, 1945, 221–248. One need not agree with White's evolutionism to agree that there are more than two ways to interpret cultural phenomena.

9. These two notions of understanding were first explicitly separated and analyzed by Jane Roland Martin in her doctoral thesis. See Jane Roland, *Understanding, Explaining and Teaching History,* unpublished Ph. D. dissertation, Radcliffe College, 1961.

10. Bronislaw Malinowski, *A Diary in the Strict Sense of the Term,* Harcourt, Brace and World, New York, 1967.

11. See for example Bronislaw Malinowski, *Coral Gardens and Their Magic,* Indiana University Press, Urban, 1967. See also Clifford Geortz's discussion of this work as well as of Malinowski's *Diary* in *The New York Review of Books,* Sept. 14, 1967.

12. S. F. Nadel, *The Foundations of Social Anthropology,* Cohen & West, London, 1951, p. 18.

13. Scheffler, *op cit.*

14. Howard S. Becker and Blanche Geer, 'Participant Observation' in R. N. Adams and J. J. Preiss, *Human Organization Research*

pp. 267–289; for another attempt to distinguish different senses of participant observation see Buford H. Junker, *Field Work*, University of Chicago Press, Chicago, 1960.

15. Sir James Frazer, 'Preface' to *Argonauts of the Western Pacific*, pp. vii–viii.

16. Malinowski, *Argonauts of the Western Pacific*, p. 8.

17. John Madge, *The Tools of Social Science*, Doubleday, New York, 1965, p. 137.

18. Eric Fromm, 'Psychoanalysis and Zen Buddhism,' in Suzuki, Fromm, and DeMartino, *Zen Buddhism and Psychoanalysis*, Grove Press, New York, 1963, p.112.

19. M. Herskovits, *Life in a Haitian Valley*, New York 1937, p. 323.

20. Beattie, *op. cit.*, p. 14.

21. Florence Kluckhohn, 'The Participant Observer Technique in Small Communities,' *AJS*, 1940, 331–343.

22. Beattie, *op. cit.*, p. 47.

23. John Beattie, *Other Cultures*, The Free Press, New York, 1964, p. 87.

24. *Ibid.*, p. 82.

25. George P. Murdock, 'British Social Anthropology' *AA* 53 (1951) 465–473.

26. See Margaret Mead and Rhoda Metraux (ed.), *The Study of Culture at a Distance*, University of Chicago Press, Chicago, 1953, pp. 41–49.

27. Cornelius Osgood, 'Informants,' in *Yale University Publication in Anthropology*, 1940, pp. 50–55.

28. See Margaret Mead, 'Native Language as Field Work Tools,' *AA*, 1939, 189–205.

29. R. Larco Hoyle, *Los Mochicas*, Museo R. Larco Herrera, Trujillo (Peru), 1945.

30. Irving Rouse, 'The Strategy of Culture History,' in *Anthropology Today* (ed. by A. L. Kroeber), The University of Chicago Press, Chicago, 1953, pp. 61–62.

31. Morris Zelditch, 'Some Methodological Problems of Field Studies,' *AJS*, 1962, 566–576.

32.   For a criticism of the thesis that all anthropologists should do field work, see I. C. Jarvie, 'On Theories of Fieldwork and the Scientific Character of Social Anthropology,' *Philosophy of Science* 34 (1967) 223–242.

33.   A. L. Kroeber, *An Anthropologist Looks at History*, University of California Press, Berkeley, 1966, p. 124.

34.   See Carl R. Hausman, 'Intradiction: An Interpretation of Aesthetic Understanding,' *Journal of Aesthetics*, 1963–64, 249–261.

9

Decontextualized Meanings: Current Approaches to *Verstehende* Investigations

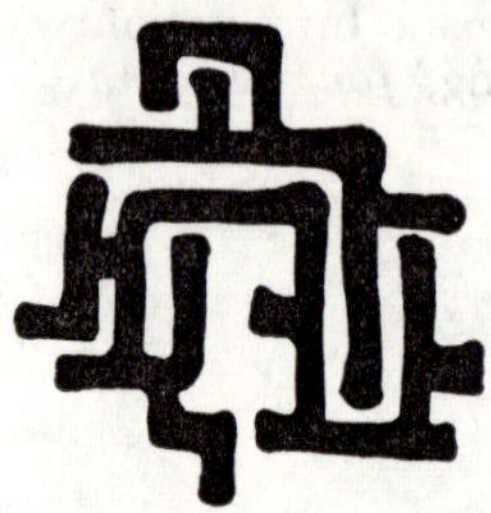

Jeff Coulter

As we have noted, much if not most of contemporary social science's concern with *verstehen* has involved its incorporation into modern positivistic methodology. In recent years, however, there has been a substantial revival of interest in the essentially philosophical questions initiated by Dilthey as to the special character of explanation within the social sciences. Most modern sociologists seem to have accepted the model for scientific explanation popular in the natural sciences which has become generally known as the "covering law" model of explanation—wherein particular events are explained through subsuming them under general laws (cf., Hempel and Oppenheim, 1948, and Braithwaite, 1953). This pattern has resulted in the popular rejection of *verstehen* as a valid form of explanation (cf., e.g., Nagel, 1953; Rudner, 1966; and Hempel, 1965).

In recent years, however, there has been a great deal of reexamination of the problems of explanation in all the sciences. This has led to the disclosure of new problems within the natural

This is an extended and slightly modified version of a paper of the same title that appeared in *The Sociological Review*, 19, No. 3, August 1971, pp. 301–323. The modifications are occasioned by a feeling that the intelligibility of the paper required them; the arguments developed in it remain unchanged in all respects. The author is grateful to the editors of *The Sociological Review* for their kind permission in allowing him to effect such changes as he thought useful. This article is reprinted here by permission of *The Sociological Review*.

sciences, and several alternative models for explanation in the social sciences have been suggested (cf., e.g., Borger and Cioffi, 1970; Gardner, 1957; Gallie, 1968; Louch, 1966; Martin, 1970; and Winch, 1958). Even though interest in unifying the methods of the social and natural sciences has continued, there has been a recognition that the problem has probably been oversimplified. As the philosopher of science, Michael Scriven, has noted:

> *There is very little in the social sciences that does not have a parallel in the physical sciences, but it has not been to these parallels that social scientists have turned for paradigms. They have turned instead to the absurdly over-simple paradigms of Newtonian mechanics and astronomy.* (Scriven, 1968, p. 90.)

From the current debate within the philosophy of science a steady but lagging input threatens to alter the widespread impression among sociologists that the *verstehen* issue has been largely laid to permanent rest. This input has been recently surveyed by Keat (1971), but its impact upon the social sciences is yet to be fully judged.

The new concern with the special character of sociological explanation has centered about the works of the phenomenological philosopher-sociologist Alfred Schutz (cf., Natanson, 1963, and Schutz, 1962) and been carried forward by many sociologists in the symbolic interactionist tradition, especially those who have taken a perspective they call *ethnomethodology* (cf., Garfinkel, 1967, and Denzin, 1969). In the following final essay, Jeff Coulter describes some of these recent new concerns with the proper role of *verstehen*.

—MT

Sociologists interested in theories of action have virtually all taken as their starting-point Weber's conception: "In action is included all human behaviour insofar as the actor attaches a subjective meaning to it."[1] There has followed from this some tendency to view action as equivalent to behaviour plus meaning, stemming from the notion of "attachment" in Weber's formulation. The observable world of events contains both actions and behaviours and the distinguishing features of actions are not hidden away in actors' subjective recesses where "meaning-attachments" are made: we manifestly see actions, and know what we see to be actions and not behaviours in every calculable sense. A description of a social scene in process which was framed in purely behavioural terms would be quite senseless as data for a sociologist. A better differentiation is, of course, to posit actions as *rule-following* conduct, as suggested by Winch.[2] In the sense that the rules of games furnish the sense of behavioural events that constitute them, we can speak of *contextual* rules governing the describable properties of human action. From the standpoint of one situated observation, recognisable actions can appear "meaningless" and yet still be seen as actions and not behaviours. Thus the identification problem becomes one of specifying the appropriate contextual properties; e.g., "X is breaking the rules of this game" pure and simple, or "X is now playing game A rather than game B." These examples are illustrative, as human interaction is viewed therein *after the fashion of games,* i.e. analogously, and not literally. This glance at one aspect of what is involved in asking for the meaning of an action—namely, its identification—must now be supplemented by other considerations. One can ask for the meaning of an action in terms of asking for the reasons that informed it; one can ask for the meaning in terms of asking for the possibly special significance of an action; in terms of asking for a statement of its place in some wider pattern of activity, etc. All of these requests may turn out to be problematic in particular instances, but posing the question in terms of some generic and epistemological issue of "meaning" tends to confuse. We need to decompose the problem into its elements. The problematics of meaning determination vary contextually, as do the grounds for deciding upon the adequacy of an answer.

A further confusion in this sphere has been introduced by Winch, who follows Wittgenstein in advising us not to ask for the meaning but to look for the usages of words if we wish to know how they function in actual linguistic practices. Winch thence proposes a similarity of task for philosophy and sociology, whereas the latter's enterprise is informed by a study of cultural rules governing usages, not logical ones.[3]

In this paper, then, I shall examine current practices in sociology and anthropology concerned with analysing social structures as meaningful human products (assembled out of communicative resources), and I will consider in particular aspects of the work of phenomenologists, ethnoscientists and Cicourel's contribution to ethnomethodology.

MODELS OF MAN

Actors have diverse methods for making operative and theoretical sense out of their perceived social environments: there are very diverse possible schemata of interpretation for the same piece of human conduct. Burke refers to these as "accounting schemes."[4] In one accounting scheme, for example, the industrial activity of communist intellectuals will be accounted for as "agitation" towards the goal of bringing about the downfall of Western democracies; in another, the same activity will be accounted for as the forging of an alliance of workers and intellectuals in order to overthrow class society and herald a libertarian socialist order. Dealing with motives, Burke establishes that any rounded statement about motive can be classified into a pentad of key terms: act, scene, agent, agency and purpose. These form resources with wide possibilities for transformation and combination over which actors will agree and disagree as to contextual applicability, generalisability and primacy. The ratios derivable from Burke's pentad are interesting. In a scene-act ratio, the background setting is conceptualised as coercive to the performance of a particular act (e.g., "living in those slums would drive anyone to crime, and X was no exception"); in a scene-agent ratio, the quality of the background is posited as the principle factor in producing the characterological "types" emergent from it. Objects, also, are differentially conceptualisable according to the terms of the pentad: a pianist may conceive of his hands as primarily *agents*, a surgeon doing an operation on an arthritic patient may regard the patient's hands in a purely materialistic light as *scenic* properties of the body, whilst a palmist would read off possible *actions* from the hands. The situational specificity of motivational accounts and the indexicality[5] of definitions of situations, projects and objects' significances remain quite irremediable.

The human sciences are not purged of common-sense rationalities such as these by virtue of their scientism. Models of man are to be found informing much theoretical work, and debates about

appropriate assumptions still consume space in the journals. What
appears notably inadequate about most sociological and psychological models is that they portray the actor as a "judgmental dope,"
in Garfinkel's terms.[6] The cultural dope acts in accordance with
the standardised, preestablished and legitimate alternatives of action provided by the common culture; the psychological dope produces society's stable features by making choices among alternative
courses of action that are compelled on grounds of psychiatric biog-
raphy, conditioning history and variables of mental functioning.
"Hierarchies of need dispositions, and common culture as enforced
rules of action, are favoured devices for bringing the problem of
necessary inference to terms, although at the cost of making out
the person-in-society to be a judgmental dope."[7] Bannister cites a
couple of prevalent specimens:

> . . . psycho-analytic theories suggest that man is essentially
> a battlefield, he is a dark cellar in which a maiden aunt and
> a sex-crazed monkey are locked in mortal combat, the affair
> being refereed by a rather nervous bank clerk. Alternatively,
> learning theory and stimulus-response psychology generally
> seem to suggest that man is essentially a ping-pong ball with
> a memory.[8]

Bolton has outlined what is involved when sociology is conceived
of as a behavioural science in terms of models of the actor,[9] and
Glaser has discussed the images underlying much contemporary
criminology,[10] whilst several commentators have pointed to, and
analysed the import of, the diverse accounting schemes currently
employed in psychiatry.[11] The essentially synecdochal nature of
each accounting scheme, or image of man, leads quite frequently to
the sort of spurious syncretism found, for example, in the marriage
of Marxism to psychoanalysis.

As there can be no generalised contexts, no all-embracing
mode of inquiry and no purge of the indexicality of accounting
schemes employed by members of a society, so there can be no
finality in the interpretations offered of socially accomplished
settings and assembled events. There *is* finality for members of
those settings and participants in those events, but it is marked
with a (generally unstated) subordinate clause or cut-off point—
for all practical purposes."[12]

Further, as sociological models have generally neglected or assumed away common-sense situations of practical choice in everyday life and the issue of how such situations are managed, they are involved in implicit reification. The search to break out of this reifying model-construction has taken two distinct directions in recent work. The first is concerned with seeking out definitive answers to the epistemologically posed "problem of meaning," the second with focusing upon formal structures of practical actions. Both claim to have learned something of importance from phenomenology, and I shall touch on this as I consider them in greater detail.

SOCIOLINGUISTIC RESOURCES FOR STUDYING MEANING

The Meadian distinction between object and stimulus lies at the heart of the sociological interest in symbolic interaction. Objects do not have any basic, invariant and intrinsic identification beyond that which is recognised in terms apposite to an actor's on-going contextual interest in them. A stimulus is a mechanical, electrical or chemical event impinging upon a perceptor organ and coercing an uninterpreted, automatic response. Human communication is inter-indication—the transmission of meaningful messages—rather than inter-stimulation. There is no intrinsic fixity about social objects (and events); contexts permitting, there is an enormous sanctioned latitude of variability in everyday life for their interpretation, definition or self-indication. The proliferation of alternative methods of organising common activities and experiences asserts a stubborn primacy over sociological efforts to provide models of invariant properties of social-action arenas, just as for Wittgenstein the vast number and diversity of *games* seemed to rule out any specification of common properties: there were simply many different language-games in which the term "game" became intelligible. This attack upon *essentialism* holds good for sociology: we cannot specify any uniform indicators for our sociological variables without violating, or rather, arbitrarily extrapolating from, common usages. However, in everyday life no exhaustive list of the properties of phenomenon X need be spelt out before "X" can be legitimately used in talk.

Courses of social action, like games, may well have *family resemblances*, but no more. Socially constructed symbolic representations can never have the boundedness or "closure" of the phenomena dealt with in the natural sciences. It is illegitimate to seek to measure social phenomena according to metrics whose axiomatic bases are in no way correspondent with the features of the phenomena. A fruitless search for generic variables with consistent indicators has led to the postulation of things called "epistemic coefficients"—measuring the relationships between the "intangible" but *real* phenomena being depicted through arbitrarily selected though related indicators in path-diagrammatic models;[13] e.g., social integration and prejudice, etc.

With this in mind, let us turn to a schematic examination of some recent work on the eliciting of meaning-structures from social situations, which sets about this task by analysing members' utterances into uniform and finite semantic components. The programme of ethnoscience is the examination of a culture's practical taxonomies and the relationship between particular ways of classifying both its material and cultural universes. The term "ethnoscience" itself is often used to refer to the totality of a culture's indigenous symbolic constructs.[14] The methodological apparatus for such an enterprise is componential analysis. This involves asking for (and sometimes observing the uses of) categories relating to such things as plants, magical rites and kinship systems, in order to assign such categories to distinctive locations in sets and sub-sets such that every item is distinguished from every other by at least one component. In this way the "native contrasts" are obtained and abstracted. There are differing views as to the utility of componential analysis of this type. The assertion that componential analysis provides "a cognitive description of a culture," in Tyler's terms,[15] has induced anthropologists to enter into serious discussion in the literature as to whether analyses revealed only the native criteria for usages from the "outside" on the basis of fragmentary evidence (and thus constituted nothing more than the imposition of the analyst's decontextualised frameworks of such criteria); or whether any models could be claimed to be in perfect correspondence with actual, native reasoning.[16] Burling raised forcefully the issues of, first, the possibility of constructing logically alternative models, each with high (or even equivalent) predictive capacity; secondly, the possibility that not all speakers utilise the same practical criteria (i.e., the same models, or "mental maps," represented in the componential constructions); and thirdly, the fact that the in-built methodological demand for *pragnanz*, or boundedness (the exclusion of possibilities of indeterminacy of category use, or "open-texture") might distort the substantive representations of actual category uses found in the cultures under study.[17]

The debate has been unfortunately phrased in terms of "structural" versus "psychological" realities, in the sense that the former represent *only* the analyst's "approximation," whilst the latter represent the cognitive structure of the natives. The notion that an anthropologist who accounts for all of his observations by formulating a series of rules is doing *other* than this—is, in fact, discovering some discrete "cognitive structure"—is based upon what Quine has referred to as the museum myth of semantics:

> Uncritical semantics is the myth of a museum in which the exhibits are meanings and the words are labels…. Semantics is vitiated by a pernicious mentalism as long as we regard a man's semantics as somehow determinate in his mind beyond what might be implicit in his dispositions to overt behaviour… even in the complex and obscure parts of language learning, the learner has no data to work with but the overt behavior of other speakers.[18]

Clearly, the notion that one can discern a realm that could be called a culture's or natives' *cognitive* system is akin to the old idea that language has an existence "out there" (or "in there"), fundamentally independent of its myriad contexts of application. There is no *essential* code of criteria that underlies every linguistic practice; there are only general conventions which are subject to the exigencies of language-users' levels of understanding, purposes and choices.

It is precisely this sort of conception of a discrete subjective province that lies behind Psathas' remark that

> Any social scientist who insists that he can understand all of man's behaviour by focussing only on that part which is overt and manifested in concrete, directly observable acts is naive, to say the least.[19]

But what else have we got—and why should we need more? (Unless our interest is directed to the behaviour of endocrine glands, etc.) Presumably to understand the meaning that the actor's act has for him requires us to do other than ask for it or make an inference— and asking for it makes it observable. [20] Actors can certainly keep secrets from us, or lie to us if they wish, but on neither score do we need to do otherwise than observe: in Garfinkel's felicitous terms, there is nothing in the head of the actor that is of interest to us; there are only brains. [21] For the componential analysts, the cognitive world of the actors observed is conceptualised as a static structure out of which situational uses and modes of conduct derive like rabbits from a conjurer's hat. The essentialism of ethnoscience is noted by Psathas, who attempts to liken it to the phenomenological search for essences, the *eidos* of experience, and whose own research exemplar is adduced to illustrate the form that it could take. In order to understand how cab-drivers locate addresses, Psathas assures us that we require a "phenomenological analysis" that would lead us to

> the essence of "location" on which are imposed, in layers of meaning, so to speak, the more unique and specific elements and relationships among elements that constitute locations for the cab driver in a particular kind of socio-cultural space, e.g., the urban environment. [22]

This passes without clarification as to what can remain "essential" in the symbolic environment of changing definitions of situation, the relativity of stance and interest, the negotiable character of social-communicative relations. Settling upon the Schutzian notion of "typifications of typifications" as a theoretical guideline, Psathas (and others) view the sociologist as the furbisher of second-order constructs. These second-order constructs are built out of the lay actors' first-order constructs with little clarity as to *how* the former are constructed in this way and what they could consist in apart from (a) different first-order constructs or (b) a spurious search for the crystalline purity of fundamental symbolic units or units of prime cultural significance that so frequently culminates in the provision of reifications of ordinary usages. Sociology in this perspective is indeed in the same predicament as pre-Wittgensteinian philosophy of the *Investigations* period, and appears currently condemned to commit the same order of mistakes. D'Andrade's equation of semantic features with hypothetical cognitive invariants[23] leads Psathas to claim that the "ethnomethods" could enable us to "know the mind of the subjects studied."[24] The strictures of both Wittgenstein and Quine inform us that this cannot be other than in the sense in which we can say of them that they do, or are disposed to do, any of a large collection of publicly observable things. Thus, to return to our original citation, we would not wish to do other than focus "only on that part [of man's behaviour] which is overt."[25]

CICOUREL ON LANGUAGE, MEANING AND MODELS

One finds in reading the work of Aaron Cicourel that three distinct layers of reality are being conceptualised as independent phenomena and counterposed in loose relationship to one another: thought, language and meanings. Witness his approving citation of Lamb:

> Phonemic systems must be adapted to speech and auditory organs, while sememic systems must be adapted to thought patterns. Moreover, the process of linguistic change affects these two strata in different ways. . . .[26]

Cicourel himself laments the fact that

> Little attention is given to the anthropologist's and sociologist's problem of connecting sound and thought patterns with cultural meanings, and with the language as it is spoken and written.[27]

Further on, he asserts that

> The actor's experience of events and objects in his environment, his thought patterns and the meanings to which they are linked are communicated via casual and noncasual language and via spoken units and written ones.[28]

What is needed, notes Cicourel in another, later volume, are

> . . . rules for moving from the actor's experience to verbal and nonverbal communication, and from an act or event or sequence of events to a description of activities that can be examined independently by other researchers.[29]

This, we are told, is what recent work in sociolinguistic and ethnomethodology is seeking to obtain. Cicourel's perspective on Witt-

genstein needs citing at this point, prior to detailed discussion of
the issues raised by the above citations. For Cicourel, Wittgenstein

> . . . appears to say that language is not in perfect correspon-
> dence either with formal logic or with everyday life meaning.
> Language and "game" have rules, but these rules are not lit-
> eral rules in the sense of exhausting a set of possibilities or
> determining a set of possible outcomes. . . . The language we
> adopt for describing the realities of life always runs the risk
> of entanglement with what we mean.[30]

An advocate of the Sapir-Whorf view of language, Cicourel
notes how language "and the cultural meanings it signifies, dis-
torts, and obliterates, acts as a filter or grid for what will pass as
knowledge in a given era. Similarly, cultural meanings . . . have
their own grammar which may be expressed and/or influenced by
language."[31] By holding to this view, Cicourel finds himself in
the same sort of predicament as Schutz—by starting from consciousness and experience and working outwards to language and
communication (in a form of implicit ontogenetic and phyloge-
netic model), the reverse of Mead's procedures, he finds himself
unable to reunite convincingly, in conceptual terms, the two
"realms" of thought and language as they take on the appearance
of discrete spheres.[32] There is no good reason to believe that language structures are barriers to concept formation—it does not
follow that those modalities of conceptualisation expressed in any
given language at any period exert restrictions upon a speaker's
freedom of conceptualisation. Burling comments, with respect to
ethnoscientific endeavours,

> The hope that we could somehow use our knowledge of lan-
> guage to gain understanding of the workings of the human
> mind has had a long history. Whorf's ideas have fallen into
> disrepute largely because the relationships which he claimed
> to see between patterns of language and patterns of thought
> could be checked only from the side of language. The lan-
> guage patterns were there to be sure, but how, except through
> intuition, could one tell whether the patterns corresponded
> to anything else?[33]

One could ask of Cicourel, as Wittgenstein did in a similar
case, "Are you sure . . . that [X] is the correct translation of your
wordless thought into words?"[34] The same could be asked of

Habermas' "paleo-symbols"—the introjected, pre-linguistic enti-
ties that are somehow externalised, made "scenic," in psychoan-
alytic encounters.[35] Issues pertaining to the individual possession
of certain *concepts*, even types of knowledge, are being confused
with issues pertaining to language as the totality of a culture's
functioning usages. Language is a medium of expression.

Let us concentrate upon the three phenomena we claimed
earlier were being misunderstood: thought, language and meanings. Consider language generally. The words in a language, developed out of vocal gestures, are best seen as tools, or counters in
heteroclitic language-games, without any essential foundation underlying diverse usages. Asking questions about language and its structure in abstraction from the contextual usages of words in that
language leads to the fallacy of assuming that the answers lie *behind* the usages. The concepts that are involved in language-games
settle for us the form of our experiences of the world: they are
the tools of thought. Language itself can never distort or restrict,
can never be true or false, but can only be a resource for constructing meaningful or meaningless communications; permitting intelligible or unintelligible usages in contexts. Language, and the concepts articulated therein, is the medium or vehicle of thought.
Thought is the non-articulated manipulation of lingual symbols,
and is wholly emergent from the development of vocal gestures.[36]
It is made up of the same stuff as language: the nature of both
Lamb's and Cicourel's "thought-patterns" remains quite obscure,
detached as they appear to be from "meanings" (even from "language as it is spoken and written"[37]) or, in Lamb's formulation, detached from sememic systems whose relationship to them is apparently problematic. If one remembers the phenomenological
point that one never experiences consciousness as a putative sub-
stratum-in-itself, only consciousness *of* something (Husserl's
noemata), one can begin to cease conceptualising thought as
something *other than* non-articulated lingual manipulation that
somehow comes to be "linked to," or attached to "meanings,"
etc. Meanings in the cultural sense (e.g., the sense of some observable act or utterance, grounds for inference, etc.) may well be
ambiguous and open-ended in terms of interpretation (the rules
that govern interpretations are conventions that are best conceived as analogous to signposts), but they are indubitably public

and scenic. Intentions, on the other hand, are sometimes public, sometimes private. To say that there is a public mental language with which one can talk about one's mental states (and only therein intelligibly) is *not* to say that any statement about the intention of another person strictly and deductively follows from any set of statements about the behaviour he enacts.[38] However, in everyday life, what others say and do provides all the grounds that are required for the justification of our beliefs about their intentions.

When Cicourel states that for Wittgenstein, "language is not in perfect correspondence . . . with everyday life meaning,"[39] he is presupposing an absurd disjunction that conceives of language as a self-contained system which somehow fails to accord with its particular usages. It is like saying that arithmetic is out of joint with routine calculations. Or, again, to state that it (language) is not in correspondence with formal logic[40] is to forget that logic is a codification of the rules governing correct inferences. Language is not a realm with mathematically specifiable relationships, a fixed calculus lurking like a skeleton behind the contingencies of everyday discourse. Rather, it is a polymorphous array of living, working conventions with immense elasticity and combinatorial resources. Cicourel appears to speak of language as something other than sound, thought and cultural meanings, and he theoretically hives off an actor's thought processes from meanings (here it is left unclear as to what sense of that ubiquitous term "meaning" is intended), and both from communication, with all three coupling up like rail carriages to form the language train.[41]

In his demand for general rules for moving from actors' experiences to communication,[42] Cicourel leaves one wondering what sort of rules these could be, what form they could take. Expressions relating to experience are contextually intelligible or they are not—if I want to know about someone's particular experience of something, I ask him about it, eliciting a move from experience to public communication. As experiences are symbolically or conceptually constituted, there are no inherent difficulties in "translation" to public talk about them, although problems might arise if an actor fails to articulate an account of them to either his or my satisfaction. Then both speaker-hearers must find a way to lock into an appropriate rule for communicating the topic in hand. As Garfinkel puts it,

> "Shared agreement" refers to various social methods for
> accomplishing the member's recognition that something was
> said-according-to-a-rule and not the demonstrable matching
> of substantive matters. The appropriate image of a common
> understanding is therefore an operation rather than a common
> intersection of overlapping sets.[43]

Interpretations of such rules would always leave latitude for various
other possible formulations, since, as Dummett has noted:

> It is undoubtedly true and important that, while in using a
> word or symbol we are in some sense following a rule, this
> rule cannot in its turn be formulated in such a way as to
> leave no latitude in its interpretation, or, if it can, the rules
> for using the words in terms of which this rule is formulated
> cannot in their turn be so formulated.[44]

Criteria for assessing the adequacy of a rule formulation vary contextually. Cicourel's programme aims at providing *decontextualised coding-rules for human experience and decontextualised
rules of inference.* This departs from the programme of ethnomethodology insofar as part of the latter's concern is with

> Not *a* method of understanding, but immensely various meth-
> ods of understanding [as] the professional sociologist's
> proper and hitherto unstudied and critical phenomena.[45]

Elsewhere Cicourel remarks how little information we have as to
how "the actor in everyday life" employs gestures, body motions,
ecological cues, intonation and grammatical structures, etc., to
make sense of his environment: "Nor is it clear how scientific observers of social settings accomplish the same activities according to
scientific rules of procedure that *any man* can follow."[46] Such
"scientific rules of procedure" remain a mystery, and the emphasis
of the remark (on "the actor ... ") indicates that what is required
is some general theory of what are through and through contextual
matters. Further, the theory demands that both actor and scientist be conceived in terms of "contructed types."[47] Schutz's pup-
pet-like homunculus[48] manipulated by the social scientist bears a
closer resemblance to *Homo economicus* than to *Homo sociologicus* in current theorising, as any model of *Homo sociologicus* could
only be assembled out of extrapolations from real human action
scenes. He is the product of concentrating upon one especially favoured corner of the patterns of human activity to the detriment

of concern with the other patterns revealed by a less restricted inquiry; i.e., the product of a clearly synecdochal approach. Such an approach is a document of sociology's continual desire for warrantable generalisations about human conduct; generalisations that transcend the actually witnessed evidences without recourse to the inevitable crudities of statistical methods. The forging of abstract, decontextualised and invariant models of actors' "meaning-structures" is a reaction as positivistic in intent as the forging of Humean causal or probabilistic laws of social action. Are we thus committed to a picture of meaning as "a situational fiction because use changes continuously"?[49] Cicourel raises this question and cites Ziff's work on syntax and semantics [50] in order to assert the relevance of observations and analyses of syntax for the study of meanings in talk. But he fails to demonstrate the connection—a particularly noteworthy exclusion as he previously cites Chomsky's statement: "I think we are forced to conclude that grammar is autonomous and independent of meaning,"[51] and he himself comments that the grammaticalness of a questionnaire does not ensure that the subjects being questioned will perceive and interpret the questions posed in the same way as does the sociologist.[52] In fact, this is posed as a general issue, whereas it might more readily be conceived as an occasional difficulty short of extra-communicative criteria for the assessment of whether or not an actor "has really understood what is presented to him in the manner intended by the investigator as evidenced in his talk about it"—a lack of such criteria is given in the human condition. Without such criteria we make the mistakes we do and are fallible in a way that we could not be if we had access to such metaphysical failsafes. If we wish to make assertions about people's activities on the basis of sampled questionnaires, then we can expect to be wrong much of the time. It is not that we can sharpen up our questionnaire construction procedures to avoid mistakes; rather, we can choose alternative methodologies for the investigation of human group life. There are no final arbiters—only our faculties of observation. Existence *from within* a culture is the bedrock from which any science, sociology included, must commence, even when our cultural resources become our topics.

MEANINGS AND NOMINALISM

Weber writes about "attachments" of meaning, Cicourel about the "assignation" of meaning and Blumer[53] about "conferral" of meaning. All of these ways of talking about *meaning* can dispose a student to view the process of interpretation on the part of actors as analogous to a nominalist practice—the arbitrary labelling of objects and actions. To correct this it may be useful to assert that neither static, common properties coerce labels from observers, nor do purely capricious idiosyncracies suffice as organising principles in a culture: rather, it is customary conventions that decide whether or not some phenomenon (in the social and physical worlds) has been accurately or inaccurately classified (i.e. labeled).[54] There are no further, finite resolutions to any ambiguities that might arise:

> Suppose an expedition comes back from the headwaters of the Amazon bearing specimens of a hitherto unsuspected species of creatures, black and hairy, with the looks and habits of a tarantula, but having only six legs: using the word "spider" in the ordinary way, how should we describe this find? Should we say, "here, surprisingly enough, is a six-legged spider"; or should we say, "here is a creature very like a spider, but it isn't a spider because it hasn't eight legs"? ... The everyday use of the word "spider" is not sharp in this respect. It is not precisely settled in ordinary language ... All we can say is that in the light of our past use of the term (we could be justified in saying either).[55]

It is worth emphasising that our common usages furnish us with sufficiently clear contrasts—for practical purposes—so that when a man misidentifies or misdescribes a smile as a frown, we can tell that he has "assigned the wrong meaning" to the phenomenon. Similarly, it is not that a fluttering cloth attached to a pole over a high building is merely labelled a "flag"—it *is* a flag. Nominalists are correct to point out that human interests and purposes play a large part in determining which principles of classification we choose, but this does not mean that any principles will necessarily suffice if intelligibility is to be preserved in discourse. There may be a limitless number of *possible* classification systems, but there is only a finite number of *actual* conventions operable in human societies. Statements of such conventions are, again, bound up with practical purposes for their "adequacy" of formulation.

One can perhaps discern in this the difficulties with operationalism: the equation of arbitrarily selected measurable properties with real, qualitatively distinct phenomena—a purely nominalist practice. Take Osgood's operationalisation of "meaning" for purposes of measurement:

> Within the general framework of learning theory, we have identified this cognitive state, *meaning*, with a representational mediation process and have tried to specify the objective stimulus and response conditions under which such a process develops.[56]

Because it is deemed methodologically necessary for Osgood and his colleagues to re-draft the concept of "meaning" into stimulus-response terms, it becomes a fixed property of specific referrents. (One might add that the nature of such referrents is obscure—in what sense is "meaning" conceivably a "state," let alone a cognitive one?) The semantic differential technique follows a procedure whereby a concept is to be differentiated by a subject against a set of adjectives. This is then held to denote a mapping, or measurement, of actual cognitive organisation *in* the subject. The distinction involved in this approach between our natural and technical language is such as to rule out any correspondence between what we normally understand by "meanings" and what is purported to be measured here. In a similar vein, Kelly's Personal Construct approach is heralded as a "new measure of personality."[57] It involves the statistical sorting of relationships between conceptual categories, wherein the subject must align categories to systems of classification. From this the analyst deduces a model of the subject's personality "traits"—a series of reifications constructed on the basis of the circumscribed operations of an experimental situation. Redefinitions of commonly used concepts are adduced formally to substantiate the claims of the approach; e.g., anxiety is redefined as "the awareness that the events with which one is confronted lie mostly outside the range of convenience of one's construct system";[58] and guilt is asserted to be "the awareness of dislodgement of the self from one's core role structure."[59] It is clear that neither anxiety nor guilt have such generic qualities in everyday life, and that these definitions, if they hold for any instances, do not hold for a vast variety of socially sanctionable and contextually specifiable usages. (One is often anxious or guilty *about* something, in ways that differ according to what it is that one feels anxious or guilty about.) Such procedures as Osgood's and Kelly's are based upon the positivistic demand for "hard" data (i.e., quantitative and potentially predictive) from what turn out to be diverse descriptors of experience whose uses are in perpetual contextual flux.

Coercing disparately qualitative phenomena into prematurely conceived mathematical moulds is the contemporary stock-in-trade of scientism—its rhetorical tropes include a vast armoury of operationalised constructs that can never be used to tell us about the *nature* of what has been operationalised.[60] Cicourel, despite his apparent ambivalence over the possibility of measurement,[61] has severely undercut demographic sociology's claims to provide rigorous knowledge of social structures. Macrosociological work, it appears, is necessarily bound up with theoretical crudities, and the switching of attention to extremely small-scale studies of formal structures of practical, everyday activities announced by the ethnomethodologists is a departure from concentration upon large-scale sociopolitical phenomena. The inception of the latter was tied up with sociology's historical connection with social engineering and social utopianism. The nature of the macro-sociological variables such as "bureaucracy," "class," "urbanism," and "organisation" is problematic, since these terms are current throughout a speech community and feature in members' usages, in contradistinction to the descriptive armoury of the physicist or biochemist whose data are neutral with regard to how they are described and measured. Treating social constructs on a par with physical objects and events, and taking the statistical products of social organisations without considering the mass of judgmental work that goes into their production for specific purposes, involve the sociological demographer in a largely unexamined unilateralism with respect to the interpretation of both the selected "variables" and the "literality" of the quantitative representations supplied by social agencies, be they hospitals, local government departments or police bureaux. Ethnomethodology, by choosing to concentrate upon the very resources that formal sociology takes for granted in the conduct of its investigations, makes its topics the rational properties of indexical expressions, the modalities of use and comprehension of natural-languages and the artful conduct of routine affairs.

RULES AND HUMAN CONDUCT

It has long been a commonplace to observe that human beings *construct* their social orders rather than give rise to them as epiphenomenal to merely living. The mechanism whereby this work of construction is achieved is alleged to be the establishment of continual consensus over normative constraints and expectations. However, norms as such have generally been posited in a logic of exteriority—they have rarely been claimed as features of observed action scenes, but rather formulated so abstractly as to be portrayed in suspension in social space. With the concept of *rule*, sociologists have more recently attempted to locate and describe actors' definitions of situations in terms of rule-following conduct. In McHugh's terms, "describing rules as assumptions that actors make is to move a step toward description of definition, because it is now *possible* that an actor will *use* them in ways that can be observed."[62] Garfinkel's notion of "constitutive rules" of interaction forms part of an attempt to account for the regularity and stability of concerted activities. These rules are not determinative, but sense-bestowing; it is only by making reference to them that one can tell what is going on in the first place.[63] Garfinkel's notion of "preferential rules" in interaction is equivalent to, say, a manual of skills of preferred play. As Wittgenstein pointed out, the rules of tennis do not specify how hard one is to hit the ball, although there might be a different set of rules to govern that. To contravene the first set of (constitutive) rules is to create an anomic situation of utter senselessness, whilst to contravene the second set of (preferential) rules is to risk sanctions.[64] Rules are oriented to as situations are defined. Problems in defining situations, in coming to a common understanding, derive from an inability to read off the appropriate cultural rules for the observed situation. The interpretation of the rules is taken for granted by members of a society, but interpretive problems arise as no rules exhaust all possible contingencies. *Ad hoc* practices are invoked for the specification of what falls under the jurisdiction of some rule, as Garfinkel found from his work on coding, even where rules are formulated with the greatest attention paid to elaborated explicitness.[65] In the actual practice of locating constitutive rules, one has to attend to the difference between what one takes as a *criterion* for a rule's being oriented to and followed, and what may be mere *symptoms*.[66] This problem arises because one can always adduce a rule *ad hoc* to cover some performance, as long as one is allowed to construct a sufficiently specific rule.[67] This, in my view, has not as yet been fully explored in ethnomethodological work on rule use.

One example of a formal property of practical activity that Garfinkel has outlined is the documentary method of interpretation, a notion taken from Karl Mannheim,[68] which involves detecting homologous patterns of cultural meaning in very many disparate instances of situated meaning. (Denzin has mistakenly viewed this method as ethnomethodology's main programme for sociological research [69] whereas it is a discovery of an invariant property of *all* modes of practical reasoning from which the sociologist could not escape if he tried.)

In routine conversations and activities it transpires that either one must wait to see what will happen, or one must impute history and prospects by invoking tacit knowledge, in order to make sense of (get the "meaning" of) contemporaneous events. Underlying patterns of sense are derived from the individual, ongoing documents or evidences of that sense, whilst these are in turn elaborated by "what is presumed" about the underlying patterns. (As McHugh has indicated,[70] it is the operation of the documentary method of interpretation of social events that enables actors to connect up past, present and future in a social metric.)

Another feature of members' practices noted by Garfinkel is referred to as their "reflexivity":

> . . . members' accounts, of every sort, in all their logical
> modes, with all of their uses, and for every method of
> their assembly are constituent features of the settings they
> make observable. [71]

Symbolic interactionism has tended to handle actors' accounts in too abstract a manner, attempting to warrant *one* specific interpretation of social scenes by distilling it from a composite or mosaic of actors' own accounts and their interpretive work. Giving accounts, descriptions and reasons, etc., not only depends upon but contributes to the maintenance of stable routines of conduct in organised settings. Members' methods of producing "correct" (i.e., sanctionable) decisions about matters of normal practice are based upon continuing *studies* of those same settings. Garfinkel evidences this point in his analysis of an inter-sexed person managing (as a "practical methodologist") to "prove" her gender in ordinary settings. [72] It is precisely a *practical sociological reasoning* (that gains its objectivity for members according to socially organised contexts of its deployment) which enables us all to build up from fragments, passing remarks, vague categories of experience and other assorted bits and pieces of talk and appearance, a working model of social structure(s) as appropriate grounds for inference and action. The attention of the sociologist is drawn to the analysis of how members' "knowledge" gets translated into settings where matters of vital concern about fact, cause, "what happened," etc. are issues; for example, in the ethnomethodologically researched exemplars of suicide prevention centres investigating mode of death *post facto*, of jurors deciding upon a verdict, coders dealing with organisational records, police officers deciding upon the application of the label "delinquent" and so on. Members' methods of solving the methodological problems of practical sociological reasoning are now topics rather than purely resources.

REMARKS ON DESCRIPTION

Given that one cannot import into practically organised arenas any pre-established, strict rules for interpreting their features (unless one is prepared to multiply the communicative troubles from the outset), assuming the "face validity of the manifest lexical content of a message"[73] has been proposed as sufficient for survey and coding work in the social sciences (although, whilst this has been taken to mean that such a practice obviates the necessity of any kind of hermeneutic work, it nonetheless implicates the researcher in a tacit hermeneutic of his own.) On the other hand, formality about what one might previously have taken for granted semantically in reading or hearing a communication tends to multiply the features of the task—the enterprise branches out and extends the interpretable issues. Sacks asks:

How could one, then, simply by reading a variety of descriptions, decide which had a better correspondence, i.e., which was "more sociological"? Obviously, the accreditation of the authors provides no reasonable solution. Nor does the appending of a methods section, for it is given in the recognition of the etcetera problem, that if application of "the same methods" does not produce "the same description" this does not reflect on either (a) the actual methods used, or (b) the reporting of the methods. It is obviously no solution to use "the author's purpose" or for that matter the reader's purpose in reading the paper to decide adequacy of description. That merely shifts the question of using correspondence to establish adequacy from (a) correspondence between description and intended object to (b) correspondence between purpose, description and intended object. We still face a problem of reconciliation. Only now we are saying that somebody's *satisfaction* constitutes adequate grounds for his colleagues' satisfaction. . . . [74]

Sacks goes on to speculate that Weber's concern, shared by most modern sociologists, with "practical problems" of social life can be accounted for on the basis of their doubts that sociological descriptions have a cumulative character. The "etcetera problem" mentioned above in the citation refers quite simply to the fact that actors in everyday life adduce descriptions of social scenes and social events that do not pretend to display in correspondence all possible aspects of the phenomena described. There comes a cut-off point, an "etc." particle, that is socially sanctioned as a legitimate device for terminating a particular account, given that it could ramify indefinitely. Literal descriptions of social objects and events cannot attain the status of the mathematically related specifications of physical objects and events developed in the natural sciences because of the problem of correspondence and the etcetera clause. Inasmuch as this is the case, sociology competes with common-sense descriptions of society with no clear analytical warrant for its claims to scientific superiority over the latter. The import of Sacks' and Garfinkel's work is to switch from an indulgence in this sort of competition and focus upon members' interpretive procedures themselves as objects of theoretic interest.

Ethnographic materials reveal as many rich ambiguities as those found by William Empson in his work on literary classics,[75] and it seems doubtful whether the sociologist has any privileged access into matters of hermeneutic interest via the structural semantic backdoor. Concise statements of the ways in which elements of members' accounts *do* sometimes seem ambiguous may prove fruitful in helping us to overcome the problem of hearing-partisanship in hermeneutic work. This, at least, is one way of approaching the available materials. The enterprise of *verstehende* sociology has taken some interesting forms, but the emergence of ethnomethodological studies might indicate a quite decisive move to grapple with the recurring problems of delivering rigorous theoretical knowledge of actors' social structures as human constructions.

CONCLUSION

In this paper I have tried to outline some developments in social science concerned with the investigation of man as a cognitive, symbol-using, world-producing being (the *verstehende* approach) rather than as either a behaving organism, a co-ordinate in a demographer's chart or a reified factor in human ecology. Such work has travelled far since the "empathic introspectionism" of Dilthey. We are now clearly aware of the centrality of human communication for our researches, although I feel that there have been a number of misunderstandings of how this recognition can assist us. The growing interest in ethnomethodological studies might be a harbinger of a further move from the Durkheimian programme for structural sociology, but it must be borne in mind that ethnomethodology sustains a rigid theoretical indifference to the foci of other schools, given that its topics are radically distinct, and it might perhaps be time that we ceased to argue about the relative merits of each in terms of the construction of a sociological *science*, and got on with the work of building sociological theory on firmer methodological foundations (instead of the kind of philosophical issues that have been the concern of the present paper).

NOTES

1. Max Weber: *The Theory of Social and Economic Organisation* (Ed., T. Parsons), Free Press, Glencoe, 1966, p. 88.

2. Peter Winch: *The Idea of a Social Science and Its Relation to Philosophy,* Routledge and Kegan Paul, London, 1958.

3. This was pointed out to me by Dr. John Lee. I have profited from many discussions at the University of Manchester with Drs. W. W. Sharrock (who contricuted critical remarks on the first draft of this paper) and J. Lee.

4. Kenneth Burke: *A Grammar of Motives*, George Braziller Inc., New York, 1955, pp. x-xvi.

5. 'Indexicality' depicts the context-specificity of members' speech practices and processes of interpretation ('by reason of their being features of the socially organised occasions of their use' - Harold Garfinkel: *Studies in Ethnomethodology*, Prentice-Hall, Englewood Cliffs, 1967, p. 4.) The interesting properties of in-dexical expressions are more fully explored in H. Garfinkel and H. Sacks: 'On Formal Structures of Practical Actions,' in J. C. McKinney and E. A. Tiryakian (Eds.): *Theoretical Sociology: Perspectives and Developments*, Appleton-Century-Crofts, New York, 1970, pp. 327–336.

6. Harold Garfinkel: 'Studies of the Routine Grounds of Everyday Activities,' in his *op cit.*, 1967, pp. 66–8.

7. *Ibid.*, p. 68.

8. D. Bannister: 'A New Theory of Personality,' in Brian M. Foss (Ed.): *New Horizons in Psychology*, Penguin, Harmondsworth, 1966, p. 363.

9. C. D. Bolton: 'Is Sociology a Behavioral Science?,' in J. G. Manis and B. N. Meltzer (Eds.): *Symbolic Interaction*, Allyn and Bacon, Boston, 1967.

10. D. Glaser: 'Criminality Theories and Behavioral Images,' in *ibid.*

11. Anselm Strauss, Leonard Schatzman, Rue Bucher *et al.*: *Psychiatric Ideologies and Institutions*, Free Press, Glencoe, 1964.

12. See also Garfinkel's discussion of the 'etcetera clause' in *op. cit.*, 1967, pp.73 *et passim.*

13. Otis D. Duncan, H. Blalock, R. W. Hodge and others have adapted Sewell Wright's path models for dealing with population genetics to sociology in some recent papers in the *American Journal of Sociology*. The attempt is to derive causal models from correlation matrices.

14. W. C. Sturtevant: 'Studies in Ethnoscience,' *American Anthropologist*, 66, 2, 1964; A. K. Romney and R. G. D'Andrade

(Eds.): *Transcultural Studies in Cognition,* Social Science Research Council, USA, 1964.

15.   S. Tyler (Ed.): 'Introduction', in *Cognitive Anthropology,* Holt, Rinehart and Winston, New York, 1969.

16.   Anthony F. C. Wallace: 'The Problem of the Psychological Validity of Componential Analyses'; and Robbins Burling: 'Cognition and Componential Analysis: God's Truth or Hocus-Pocus?' both in S. Tyler (Ed.): *op. cit.,* 1969, pp. 396–428. Charles O. Frake, in his paper entitled, 'The Ethnographic Study of Cognitive Systems' (also in Tyler's collection, pp. 28–41) claims that 'a strategy of ethnographic description that gives a central place to the cognitive processes of the actors involved will contribute reliable cultural data (. . .) and, finally, it will give us productive descriptions which, like the linguist's grammar, succinctly state what one must know in order to generate culturally acceptable acts and utterances appropriate to a given socio-ecological context' (p.39). It seems to me that componential-analytic models cannot approach this goal, not least because, as Julius Kovesi has noted with respect to a discussion of Wittgenstein's notion of 'criterion' (in *Moral Notions,* Routledge and Kegan Paul, 1967, pp. 39–41), the features of some phenomenon do not provide us with the rules for the use of a word, 'and so it is misleading to think that they are the criteria for the proper use of a word' (p. 41). Burling, for example, notes the problem of 'indeterminacy' in connection with the language-game of *classification* ('What is the essential 'cognitive' difference between hemlock and spruce? Is it gross size, type of needle, form of bark, or what?' – *op. cit.,* p. 425) but does not go on to relate this issue to the larger issue of the variety of language-games that feature uses of these words and for which no account of the 'recognitors' (Kovesi) of the phenomena would assist us in formulating the rules of correct use applicable there.

17.   R. Burling: *op. cit.*

18.   W. V. Quine; *Ontological Relativity and Other Essays,* Columbia University Press, 1969, pp. 27–8. Further, Quine remarks: 'Seen according to the museum myth (of semantics), the words and sentences of a language have their determinate meanings. To discover the meanings of the native's words we may have to observe his behaviour, but still the meanings of the words are supposed to be determinate in the native's mind, his mental museum, even in cases where behavioural criteria are powerless to discover them for us.' (*ibid.,* p. 29).

19.   George Psathas: 'Ethnomethods and Phenomenology,' *Social Research,* 35, 3, 1968, p. 510.

20.   The error of privatism and mentalism alike is that I cannot have X's intentions, whereas all I want to know, and can frequently ascertain, is *what* X's intentions are. The sophisticated use of informants, eliciting techniques and deception devices, along with the creation of trust, are the hallmarks of artful fieldwork.

21.   Harold Garfinkel: 'A Conception of, and Experiments with, "Trust" as a condition of Stable Concerted Actions,' in O. J. Harvey (Ed.)*: Motivation and Social Interaction,* Ronald Press, New York, 1963.

22.   G. Psathas: *op. cit.,* p. 515.

23.   R. G. D'Andrade: 'Introduction,' *American Anthropologist,* 66,2, 1964.

24.   G. Psathas: *op. cit.,* p. 519.

25.   *Ibid.,* p. 510 (See note 19).

26.   Sidney M. Lamb: *Outline of Stratificational Grammar,* Associated Students of the University of California Bookstore, Berkeley, 1962, cited in Aaron V. Cicourel: *Method and Measurement in Sociology,* Free Press, New York, 1964, p. 173.

27.   A. V. Cicourel: *op. cit.,* 1964, p. 174.

28.   *Ibid.,* p. 178.

29.   Aaron V. Cicourel: *The Social Organisation of Juvenile Justice,* John Wiley and Sons, New York, 1968, p. 5.

30.   A. V. Cicourel: *op. cit.,* 1964, p. 186.

31.   *Ibid.,* p. 35.

32.   Cf. the perspective of R. E. Palmer (Hermeneutics, Northwestern University Press, 1969): 'Language is not man's means of putting wordless thoughts and wordless experience into a form to which he has assigned a meaning; thinking, understanding and experience are all completely linguistic, for it is through language that one has the world of understanding through which objects take their place in his experience. Nor is language something that can be invented; only in the most artificial situation is any word 'assigned' a meaning' (p. 230). Fred W. Householder, in his book *Linguistic Speculations* (Cambridge University Press, 1971) makes a similar observation about the relationship of language to thought. On p. 22 he writes: 'If we are not to be caught in an infinite re-

gress, we cannot suppose that speaking is a kind of translation (as is often done); we think some profound thought (in an unknown form) and then 'code' it or translate it from the unknown form into English. If this were so, then it is difficult to imagine what the underlying form of thought could be but another language–one, alas, inaccessible to study, but about which we could ask again how thoughts are put into this form. . . . Consequently we must suppose that (excluding various pictorial images and vague feelings, beliefs or expectations) thoughts are created *along with* their linguistic shape.'

33.   R. Burling; *op. cit.*, p. 426. Burling is, of course, far from denying the truth of the thesis that thought and speech are two aspects of the same process of symbolisation – he is drawing attention to the problem of checking our assertions that grammatical patterns constrain or determine speakers' world-pictures. If we *were* cognitively imprisoned in our grammars, then the problem arises as to how something like the Whorfian thesis could ever have been derived.

34.   Ludwig Wittgenstein: *Philosophical Investigations* (trans. G. E. M. Anscombe), Basil Blackwell, Oxford, 1968, para. 342, p.109e.

35.   Jurgen Habermas: 'On Systematically Distorted Communication,' *Inquiry,* 13, 3, Autumn 1970. E.G., 'The privatism of prelinguistic symbol-organisation, so striking in all forms of speech pathology, originates in the fact that the usual distance between sender and addressee . . . has not yet been developed' (p. 213). This conception differs from most versions of the private-language myth (on which, see R. Rhees: 'Can there be a Private Language?' *Proceedings of the Aristotelian Society,* Supp. Vol. XXVIII, 1954, pp. 77–94) in that here the privatism is *pre-linguistic.* However, if it is pre-linguistic, how are we to consider it as 'organised' in any sense? How would that be recognised? In his attempt to marry Freud with contemporary communication theory, Habermas seems to me to be confusing issues at several levels.

36.   I am referring in this to conceptual thinking. The fact that deaf-mutes may be said to think in some sense does not undercut the assertion that thinking must involve some kind of covert symbol-manipulating activity, and for speaker-hearers that activity is *lingual*-symbol manipulation. We yield to the syntactic and semantic structure of our language when we express internal thoughts just in the way we do in expressing them outwardly in public communication. (See above, note 32).

37. See note 27.

38. A. M. Quinton: 'Contemporary British Philosophy,' in George Pitcher (Ed.): *Wittgenstein, The Philosophical Investigations*, Macmillan, London, 1970, p. 21.

39. A. V. Cicourel: *op cit.*, 1964, p. 186.

40. *Ibid.*

41. A. V. Cicourel: *op. cit.*, 1964, p. 174 & p. 178. (See above, notes 27 & 28).

42. A. V. Cicourel: *op. cit.*, 1968, p. 5. (See above, note 29).

43. H. Garfinkel: *op. cit.*, 1967, p. 30.

44. Michael Dummett: 'Wittgenstein's Philosophy of Mathematics,' in G. Pitcher (Ed.): *op. cit.*, p. 428.

45. H. Garfinkel: *op. cit.*, 1967, p. 31.

46. A. V. Cicourel: *op. cit.*, 1968, p. 112.

47. A. V. Cicourel: *op. cit.*, 1964, p. 222.

48. Alfred Schutz: 'Common-Sense and Scientific Interpretation of Human Action,' *Philosophy and Phenomenological Research*, 14, September 1953.

49. A. V. Cicourel: *op. cit.*, 1964, p. 180.

50. Paul Ziff: *Semantic Analysis*, Ithaca, New York, Cornell University Press, 1960.

51. Noam Chomsky: *Syntactic Structures*, Mouton and Co., The Hague, 1957, p. 17, cited in A. V. Cicourel: *op. cit.*, 1964, p.174. Chomsky does not rule out some theory of language concerned with the points of connection between syntax and semantics, however, but in this early volume (the only one to which Cicourel had access at time of writing *Method and Measurement*), Chomsky noted that the consistency of usage of grammatical devices is not sufficient for us to be able to impute consistent meanings directly to them (Chomsky, p. 108). Grammars are the media for conveying meaningful messages, but the medium is very rarely the message.

52. A. V. Cicourel: *op. cit.*, 1964, p. 175.

53. Herbert Blumer: 'Society as Symbolic Interaction' in J. G. Manis and B. N. Meltzer, *op. cit.*, p. 141 and *passim*.

54. Renford Bambrough: 'Universals and Family Resemblances' in G. Pitcher (Ed.): *op. cit.*, pp. 186–204. Bambrough notes suc-

cinctly that 'The question "Are resemblances ultimate or are properties ultimate?" is a perverse question if it is meant as one to which there must be a simple, *single* answer. . . . The craving for a single answer is the logically unsatisfiable craving for something that will be the ultimate terminus of explanation and will yet itself be explained' (p. 204).

55.   Stephen F. Barker: *Philosophy of Mathematics,* Prentice-Hall, Englewood Cliffs, 1964, p. 11.

56.   C. E. Osgood, G. J. Suci and P. H. Tannenbaum: *The Measurement of Meaning,* University of Illinois Press, Urbana, 1957, p. 9, cited in A. V. Cicourel: *op. cit.,* 1964, p. 183.

57.   G. Kelly: *The Psychology of Personal Constructs,* Norton, New York, 1955, Vols. 1 & 2, cited in D. Bannister: *op. cit.*

58.   *Ibid.,* p. 368.

59.   *Ibid.*

60.   For two excellent reviews of operational methods in sociology, see Herbert Blumer; *Symbolic Interactionism: Perspective and Method,* Prentice-Hall, 1969 and Andrew J. Weigert: 'The Immoral Rhetoric of Scientific Sociology,' *The American Sociologist,* 5, 2, May 1970.

61.   For some examples, note: 'I do not wish to imply that socio-cultural events cannot be measured by existing mathematical formulations, but that the fundamental events of social action should be clarified before imposing measurement postulates with which they may not be in correspondence' (A. V. Cicourel: *op. cit.,* 1964, p. 2); 'I wish here simply to suggest possible strategies which measurement in sociology might follow. . . .' (*ibid.,* p. 179); 'On this issue depends the precise identification of the fundamental units of social analysis and the determination of their measurement properties' (p. 203); and '. . . measurement in sociology at the level of social process cannot be rigorous without solutions to the problems of cultural meanings' (p. 173). However, the import of Cicourel's first chapter appeared, to my understanding, to be directly and decisively damaging to any kind of measurement system at all as they are founded upon axiomatic bases and it is exactly this property which cannot be accommodated to social processes with any close 'fit'. One is left wondering also what 'fundamental units of social analysis' could look like, short of arbitrary abstractions from interactional episodes. Sorokin's critique of Parsons' 'unit act' is apposite in this connection. (P. A. Sorokin:

Sociological Theories of Today, Harper International, New York, 1960). These notions of Cicourel's appear to derive from his pre-occupation with treating ethnomethodological work as propaedeutic to the construction of more rational sociological methods for larger scale research. Garfinkel appears to disclaim this sort of interest and strategy in his comments in R. J. Hill and K. S. Crittendon (Eds.): *Proceedings of the Purdue Symposium on Ethnomethodology*, Purdue Research Foundation, 1968.

62.   Peter McHugh: *Defining the Situation. The Organisation of Meaning in Social Interaction*, Bobbs-Merrill, New York, 1968, p. 17. On p. 135 of this volume, McHugh asserts the possibility of the sociologist constructing 'hard' rules out of those observed, by him, in courses of interaction. It is unclear what would differentiate the two sets of rules, and why the sociologist's should be considered as 'hard' (and, by implication, the actors' as 'soft'). We seem to be back with Schutz's 'typifications', or 'second-order constructs' in a context where they are hardly appropriate.

63.   Harold Garfinkel: *op. cit.*, 1963. By grasping the constitutive (contextual) rules of a display of behavioural events, we can perceive them as potentially sensible activities; that is, they are seen not simply as physical movements but as movements in some action or patterned sequence of activities. However, as Hubert Schwyzer has noted in his paper, 'Rules and Practices' in *The Philosophical Review*, 78, 1969, p. 467: 'Rules (constitutive rules) do not themselves specify how the behaviour in accordance with those rules is to be regarded; that is something that the very setting up of the rules must presuppose'. If one did not know something of the things it is relevant to say and do with regard to a practice, one could not know what some performances governed by rules amounted to in cultural terms.

64.   H. Garfinkel: *op. cit.*, 1963.

65.   H. Garfinkel: 'Practical Sociological Reasoning: Following Coding Instructions,' in his *op cit.*, 1967, pp. 18–24.

66.   See Rogers Albritton's discussion of *criteria* and *symptoms* in his 'On Wittgenstein's Use of the Term "Criterion" ' in G. Pitcher (Ed.): *op. cit.*, pp. 231–250.

67.   K.-O. Apel; 'Wittgenstein und Heidegger: Die Frage nach dem Sinn von Sein und der Sinnlosigkeitsverdacht gegen alle Metaphysik,' *Phil. Jahrbuch*, 75, 1967, pp. 56–94, cited in Gerard Radnitzky: *Contemporary Schools of Metascience 11; Con-*

tinental Schools of Metascience, Akademiforlaget, Göteborg, Sweden, 1968, p. 98.

68.   Karl Mannheim: 'On the Interpretation of *Weltanschauung*,' in Paul Kecskemeti (trans. and Ed.): *Mannheim's Essays on the Sociology of Knowledge*, Oxford University Press, 1952, pp. 53-63.

69.   Norman Denzin: 'Symbolic Interactionism and Ethnomethodology: A Proposed Synthesis,' *American Sociological Review*, 34, 6, December 1969. Denzin's misinterpretation is: 'Garfinkel suggests the sociologist make use of . . . the documentary method of analysis.' Denzin also suggests that: they (i.e., symbolic interaction theory and ethnomethodology) as yet offer no firm strategies for measuring the interaction process,' and thereby shows that he has little clue of the import of either perspective in methodological terms. Blumer's 'Sociological Analysis and the "Variable"' and Garfinkel's remarks on sociological and statistical disjunction in his 'Common-Sense Knowledge of Social Structures. . .' must both be read (as representatives of both perspectives) as sharing a deep scepticism for all contemporary measurement practices used in sociological work.

70.   Peter McHugh: 'Emergence,' in *op cit.*, 1968, pp. 35-37.

71.   H. Garfinkel: *op. cit.*, 1967, p. 8, and *passim*.

72.   H. Garfinkel: 'Passing and the Managed Achievement of Sex Status in an Inter-sexed Person,' in *op cit.*, 1967, pp. 116-185.

73.   George J. Mahl: 'Exploring Emotional States by Content Analysis,' in Ithiel De Sola Pool (Ed.): *Trends in Content Analysis*, University of Illinois Press, 1959. Cicourel comments on this in *op. cit.*, 1964, p. 152.

74.   Harvey Sacks: 'Sociological Description,' *Berkeley Journal of Sociology*, 8, 1963, pp. 12-13.

75.   William Empson: *Seven Types of Ambiguity*, Chatto and Windus, London, 1930.

Bibliography

The following selected readings are relevant to the problem of *verstehen*. Essays included in this collection have been excluded from the list.

Abel, Theodore (1970), *The Foundation of Sociological Theory*. New York: Random House.

Anchor, Robert (1967), "Rickert, Heinrich," in Paul Edwards (ed.) *The Encyclopedia of Philosophy*. New York: Macmillan and Free Press.

Angell, Robert Cooley (1968), "Cooley, Charles H.," in David L. Sills (ed.), *International Encyclopedia of the Social Sciences*. New York: Macmillan and Free Press.

Aron, Raymond (1964), *German Sociology* (translated by Mary and Thomas Bottomore). New York: The Free Press of Glencoe.

Aron, Raymond (1970), *Main Currents in Sociological Thought II* (translated by Richard Howard and Helen Weaver). New York: Doubleday Anchor.

Arthur, C. J. (1968), "On the Historical Understanding," *History and Theory*, 7, 203–16.

Asch, Solomon E. (1959), "A Perspective on Social Psychology," in Sigmund Koch (ed.), *Psychology: A Study of a Science, Vol. 3. Formulations of the Person and the Social Context*. New York: McGraw Hill Book Co., 363–83.

Baar, Carl (1967), "Max Weber and the Process of Social Understanding," *Sociology and Social Research, 51,* 337–46.

Ball, Donald W. (1972), " 'The Definition of Situation': Some Theoretical and Methodological Consequences of Taking W. I. Thomas Seriously," *Journal for the Theory of Social Behavior, 2,* 61–82.

Bateson, Gregory (1967), "Cybernetic Explanation," *American Behavioral Scientist, 10* (April), 29–33.

Baybrooke, David (1965), *Philosophical Problems of the Social Sciences.* New York: Macmillan, 1–18.

Beck, Lewis W. (1949), "The 'Natural Science Ideal' in the Social Sciences," *Scientific Monthly, 68,* 386–94.

Becker, Howard, and Harry Elmer Barnes (1961), *Social Thought from Lore to Science,* third edition. New York: Dover.

Bendix, Reinhard (1968), "Weber, Max," in David L. Sills (ed.), *International Encyclopedia of the Social Sciences.* New York: Macmillan and Free Press, 1968.

Bierstedt, Robert (1937), "The Logico-Meaningful Method of P. A. Sorokin, " *American Sociological Review, 2,* 813–25.

Blumer, Herbert (1969), *Symbolic Interactionism: Perspective and Method.* Englewood Cliffs, N. J.: Prentice-Hall.

Borger, Robert, and Frank Cioffi (eds.) (1970), *Explanation in the Behavioural Sciences.* Cambridge: Cambridge University Press.

Boring, Edwin G. (1965), "The Historical Background for National Trends in Psychology: Remarks of Discussant," *Journal of the History of the Behavioral Sciences, 1, 2,* 138.

Braithwaite, R. B. (1953), *Scientific Explanation.* New York and London: Cambridge University Press.

Brandt, Richard, and J. Kim (1963), "Wants as Explanations of Actions," *Journal of Philosophy, 60,* 425–35.

Braude, Lee (1966), "Die Verstehende Soziologie: A New Look at an Old Problem," *Sociology and Social Research, 50,* 230–35.

Bruyn, Severyn T. (1966), *The Human Perspective in Sociology.* Englewood Cliffs, N. J.: Prentice-Hall, 1966.

Catton, William R., Jr. (1966), *From Animistic to Naturalistic Sociology.* New York: McGraw-Hill.

Cohen, Carl (1954), "Naturalism and the Method of Verstehen," *Journal of Philosophy, 51,* 220–25.

Cooley, Charles Horton (1930), *Sociological Theory and Social Research.* New York: Holt, Rinehart and Winston.

Coser, Lewis A. (1971), *Masters of Sociological Thought: Ideas in Historical and Social Context.* New York: Harcourt, Brace, and Jovanovich.

Cunningham, Frank U. (1967), "More on Understanding in the Social Sciences," *Inquiry, 10,* 321–26.

Danto, Arthur C., Alan Donagan, and J. W. Meiland (1966), "Symposium: Historical Understanding," *Journal of Philosophy, 63,* 566–582.

Denzin, Norman K. (1969), "Symbolic Interactionism and Ethnomethodology: A Proposed Synthesis," *American Sociological Review, 34,* 922–34.

Diesing, Paul (1966), "Objectivism vs. Subjectivism in the Social Sciences," *Philosophy of Science, 33,* 124–33.

Diesing, Paul (1972), "Subjectivity and Objectivity in the Social Sciences," *Philosophy of Social Science, 2,* 147–165.

Diquattro, Arthur W. (1972), "*Verstehen* as an Empirical Concept," *Sociology and Social Research, 57,* 32–42.

Dray, William (1954), "Explanatory Narrative in History," *Philosophical Quarterly, 4,* 15–27.

Dray, William (1957), *Laws and Explanation in History.* New York: Oxford University Press.

Gallie, W. B. (1968), *Philosophy and Historical Understanding,* second edition. New York: Schocken.

Gardner, Patrick (ed.) (1957), *Theories of History.* New York: Free Press.

Garfinkel, Harold (1967), *Studies in Ethnomethodology.* Englewood Cliffs, N. J.: Prentice-Hall.

George, Pulivelil Markos (1969), "The Model of Man and the Problem of Understanding," *Revue Internationale de Sociologie, 5,* 3, 130–40.

Gewirth, Alan (1954), "Subjectivism and Objectivism in the Social Sciences," *Philosophy of Science, 21,* 157–63.

Gidlow, Bob (1972), "Ethnomethodology—a New Name for Old Practices," *British Journal of Sociology, 23,* 395–405.

Goldenweiser, Alexander (1940), "The Relation of the Natural Sciences to the Social Sciences," in H. E. Barnes, H. Becker, and F. B. Becker (eds.), *Contemporary Social Theory.* New York: Appleton-Century, 93–109.

Goldstein, Leon J. (1961), "The Phenomenological and Naturalistic Approaches to the Social," *Methodos, 13,* No. 51–52, 225–38.

Gruner, Rolf (1967), "Understanding in the Social Sciences and History," *Inquiry, 10,* 151–63.

Hempel, Carl G. (1965), "The Concept of Rationality and the Logic of Explanation by Reasons," in *Aspects of Scientific Explanation.* New York: Free Press, 463–87.

Hempel, Carl G., and Paul Oppenheim (1948), "Studies in the Logic of Explanation," *Philosophy of Science, 15,* 135–75.

Hodges, H. A. (1952), *The Philosophy of Wilhelm Dilthey.* New York: Humanities Press.

Hodges, H. A. (1944). *Wilhelm Dilthey: An Introduction.* New York: Oxford University Press.

Hodges, H. A. (1968), "Dilthey, Wilhelm" in David L. Sills (ed.), *International Encyclopedia of the Social Sciences.* New York: Macmillan and Free Press.

Holborn, Hajo (1950), "Wilhelm Dilthey and the Critique of Historical Reason," *Journal of the History of Ideas, 11,* 93–118.

House, Floyd Nelson (1936), "Die Verstehende Soziologie," in *The Development of Sociology.* New York: McGraw-Hill Book Co., 393–402.

Isajiw, Wsevolod W. (1956), "Pitirim A. Sorokin's *Sistema sotsiologii:* A Summary," *American Catholic Sociological Review, 17,* 290–319.

Janowitz, Morris (ed.) (1966), *W. I. Thomas on Social Organization and Social Personality.* Chicago: University of Chicago Press.

Jarvie, I. C. (1970), "Understanding and Explanation in Sociology and Social Anthropology," in Borger and Cioffi, *op cit., 231–49.*

Keat, Russell (1971), "Positivism, Naturalism, and Anti-Naturalism in the Social Sciences," *Journal for the Theory of Social Behaviour, 1,* 3–17.

Kuczynski, Jurgen (1968), "Sombart, Werner," in David L. Sills (ed.), *International Encyclopedia of the Social Sciences,* New York: Macmillan and Free Press.

Kuhn, Manford (1964), "Major Trends in Symbolic Interaction Theory," *Sociological Quarterly, 5,* 61–84.

Lavine, Thelma (1953-a), "Note to Naturalists on the Human Spirit," *Journal of Philosophy, 50,* 5, 145–54.

Lavine, Thelma (1953-b), "What Is the Method of Naturalism?" *Journal of Philosophy, 50,* 5, 157–61.

Leat, Diana (1972), "Misunderstanding *Verstehen*," *The Sociological Review, 20,* 29–38.

Loemker, L. E. (1967), "Spranger (Franz Ernst), Eduard," in Paul Edwards (ed.), *The Encyclopedia of Philosophy.* New York: Macmillan and Free Press.

Lofland, John (1967), "Notes on Naturalism in Sociology," *Kansas Journal of Sociology, 3,* 45–61.

Lopata, Helena Znaniecki (1970), "On the Humanistic Coefficient," in G. P. Stone and H. A. Farberman (eds.), *Social Psychology Through Symbolic Interaction.* Waltham, Mass.: Ginn Blaisdell, 156–8.

Louch, A. R. (1963), "The Very Idea of Social Science," *Inquiry, 4,* 273–86.

Louch, A. R. (1965), "On Misunderstanding Mr. Winch," *Inquiry, 8,* 212–16.

Louch, A. R. (1966), *Explanation and Human Action.* Berkeley and Los Angeles: University of California Press.

Lundberg, George A. (1939), *Foundations of Sociology.* New York: Macmillan, 45–52.

MacCorquodale, Kenneth, and Paul E. Meehl (1948), "On a Distinction between Hypothetical Constructs and Intervening Variables," *Psychological Review, 55,* 95–107.

MacIver, R. M. (1942), *Social Causation.* Boston: Ginn and Co.

Markovic, Mihailo (1972), "The Problem of Reification and the *Verstehen-Erklären* Controversy," *Acta Sociologica 15,* 27–38.

Marquis, Don (1968), "Verstehen and Explanation," *Kansas Journal of Sociology, 4,* 79–87.

Martin, Jane R. (1970), "The Doctrine of Verstehen," in *Explaining, Understanding and Teaching.* New York: McGraw Hill, 168–93.

Martin, Michael (1972), "Explanation in Social Science: Some Recent Work," *Philosophy of Social Science, 2,* 61–81.

Martindale, Don (1960), *The Nature and Types of Sociological Theory*. New York: Houghton Mifflin.

Martindale, Don (1968), "Verstehen," in David L. Sills (ed.), *International Encyclopedia of the Social Sciences*. New York: Macmillan and Free Press.

Masur, Gerhard (1952), "Wilhelm Dilthey and the History of Ideas," *Journal of the History of Ideas,13*, 94–107.

McEwen, William P. (1963), *The Problem of Social-Scientific Knowledge*. Totowa, N. J.: Bedminster Press.

McLeod, Robert B. (1968), "Phenomenology," in David L. Sills (ed.), *International Encyclopedia of the Social Sciences*. New York: Macmillan and Free Press.

Mead, George Herbert (1934), *Mind, Self and Society*. Chicago: University of Chicago Press.

Mead, George Herbert (1938), *The Philosophy of the Act*. Chicago: University of Chicago Press.

Meltzer, Bernard N. (1959), *The Social Psychology of George Herbert Mead*. Center for Sociological Research, Western Michigan University.

Merton, Robert K. (1972), "Insiders and Outsiders: A Chapter in the Sociology of Knowledge," *American Journal of Sociology, 78, 9–47*.

Misiak, Henryk, and Virginia S. Sexton (1966), "Phenomenological Psychology," in *History of Psychology: An Overview*. New York: Grune and Stratton, 405–31.

Morgenbesser, Sidney (1968), "Scientific Explanation," in David L. Sills (ed.), *International Encyclopedia of the Social Sciences*. New York: Macmillan and Free Press.

Nagel, Ernest (1953), "On the Method of *Verstehen* as the Sole Method of Philosophy," *Journal of Philosophy, 50, 5*, 154–7.

Natanson, Maurice (1956), *The Social Dynamics of George H. Mead*, Washington, D. C.: Public Affairs Press.

Natanson, Maurice (1958), "A Study in Philosophy and the Social Sciences," *Social Research, 25*, 158–72.

Natanson, Maurice (ed.) (1963), *Philosophy of the Social Sciences: A Reader*. New York: Random House.

Passmore, John (1962–3), "Explanation in Everyday Life, in Science, and in History," *History and Theory, 2*.

Pierce, Albert (1956), "Empiricism and the Social Sciences," *American Sociological Review,21*, 135–7.

Popper, Karl R. (1960), *The Poverty of Historicism,* second edition. London: Routledge and Kegan Paul.

Porter, Jack Nusan (1970), "The Situational Perspective in Sociology," *Heuristics: The Journal of Innovative Sociology, 2,* 44–50.

Psathas, George (ed.) (1973), *Phenomenological Sociology.* New York: John Wiley and Sons.

Reck, Andrew (ed.) (1964), *Selected Writings of George Herbert Mead.* Indianapolis, Ind.: Bobbs-Merrill.

Rickman, H. P. (1960), "The Reaction against Positivism and Dilthey's Concept of Understanding," *British Journal of Sociology, 11,* 307–18.

Rickman, H. P. (ed.) (1961), *Meaning in History: W. Dilthey's Thoughts on History.* London: George Allen and Unwin.

Rickman, H. P. (1967), "Dilthey, Wilhelm," in Paul Edwards (ed.), *The Encyclopedia of Philosophy.* New York: Macmillan and Free Press.

Rudner, Richard S. (1966), *Philosophy of Social Science.* Englewood Cliffs, N. J.: Prentice-Hall.

Ryan, Alan (1970), *The Philosophy of the Social Sciences.* New York: Pantheon Books.

Schutz, Alfred (1962), *Collected Papers I: The Problem of Social Reality,* edited and with an introduction by Maurice Natanson. The Hague: Martinus Nijhoff.

Schwartz, Gary, and Don Merten (1971), "Participant Observation and the Discovery of Meaning," *Philosophy of Social Science, 1,* 279–98.

Scriven, Michael (1968), "Science II: The Philosophy of Science," in David L. Sills (ed.) *International Encyclopedia of the Social Sciences.* New York: Macmillan and Free Press.

Silvers, Ronald J. (1966), "The Logic and Meaning of the Logico-Meaningful Method," *Canadian Review of Sociology and Anthropology, 3,* 1–8.

Skinner, B. F. (1953), *Science and Human Behavior.* New York: Macmillan.

Skinner, B. F. (1963), " Behaviorism at Fifty," *Science, 140,* 951–8.

Sombart, Werber (1949), "Sociology: What It Is and What It Ought to Be—An Outline for a Noö-Sociology" (translated by F. C. Geiser), *American Journal of Sociology, 55,* 178–93.

Sorokin, Pitirim A. (1928), *Contemporary Sociological Theories.* New York: Harper.

Sorokin, Pitirim A. (1937-a), *Social and Cultural Dynamics, Vol.I.* New York: American Book Co., 3–53.

Sorokin, Pitirim A. (1937-b), "Rejoinder to Robert Bierstedt," *American Sociological Review, 2,* 823–5.

Sorokin, Pitirim A. (1946), "Reactions to Paper by David T. Lewis," in Kurt H. Wolff (ed.), *Contemporary American Contributions to the Sociology of Knowledge.* Mimeographed proceedings of a seminar on the sociology of knowledge, Department of Sociology, Ohio State University, Winter Term.

Sorokin, Pitirim A. (1947), *Society, Culture and Personality.* New York: Harper and Bros., 145–9 and 333–5.

Stebbins, Robert A. (1969), "Studying the Definition of the Situation: Theory and Field Research Strategies," *Canadian Review of Sociology and Anthropology, 6,* 4, 193–211.

Stewart, Ronald G. (1971), "Polemics, Verstehen and a Methodology for Undergraduates." Paper presented at the 46th Annual Meeting of the Southwestern Sociological Association.

Sutherland, N. S. (1959), "Motives and Explanations," *Mind, 68,* 145–59.

Tagiuri, Renato (1969), "Person Perception," in Gardner Lindzey and Elliot Aronson (eds.), *The Handbook of Social Psychology, Vol. III.* Reading, Mass.: Addison-Wesley, 395–449.

Tiryakian, Edward A. (1965), "Existential Phenomenology and the Sociological Tradition," *American Sociological Review, 30,* 674–88.

Tucker, William T. (1965), "Max Weber's *Verstehen,*" *Sociological Quarterly, 6,* 157–65.

Wann, T. W. (ed.), (1964), *Behaviorism and Phenomenology: Bases for Modern Psychology.* Chicago: University of Chicago Press.

Watkins, J. W. N. (1957), "Historical Explanation in the Social Sciences," *British Journal for the Philosophy of Science, 8,* 104–17.

Weber, Max (1947), *The Theory of Social and Economic Organization* (translated by A. M. Henderson and T. Parsons and edited by T. Parsons). New York: Oxford University Press.

Weber, Max (1949), *The Methodology of the Social Sciences* (translated and edited by E. A. Shils and H. A. Finch). New York: The Free Press.

Wilson, Thomas P. (1970), "Conceptions of Interaction and the Problem of Sociological Explanation," *American Sociological Review, 35,* 697–710.

Winch, Peter (1967), "Weber, Max," in Paul Edwards (ed.), *The Encyclopedia of Philosophy.* New York: Macmillan and Free Press.

Winch, Peter (1958), *The Idea of Social Science.* London: Routledge and Kegan Paul.

Winch, Peter (1964), "Mr. Louch's Idea of a Social Science," *Inquiry, 7.*

Winthrop, Henry (1964), "The Verstehen Claim in the Behavioral Sciences," *Review of Existential Psychology and Psychiatry, 4,* 141–57.

Young, Kimball, *The Contributions of William Isaac Thomas to Sociology.* Evanston, Ill.: Student Book Exchange, n.d. (*circa* 1963).

Zeitlin, Irving M. (1968), *Ideology and the Development of Sociological Theory.* Englewood Cliffs, N. J.: Prentice-Hall.

Znaniecki, Florian (1934), *The Method of Sociology.* New York: Holt, Rinehart and Winston, 34–89.